DEEP ROOTS

TOWARD A BIBLICAL AND THEOLOGICAL FRAMEWORK FOR CHURCH PLANTING

CHRISTIAN VOCATION IN CONTEXT: THE D. JAMES KENNEDY INSTITUTE OF REFORMED LEADERSHIP SERIES

BOOK TWO

MICHAEL A MILTON

WIPF & STOCK · Eugene, Oregon

DEEP ROOTS
Toward a Biblical and Theological Framework for Church Planting

Copyright © 2024 Michael A. Milton. All rights reserved. Except for brief quotations in critical publications or reviews, no part of this book may be reproduced in any manner without prior written permission from the publisher. Write: Permissions, Wipf and Stock Publishers, 199 W. 8th Ave., Suite 3, Eugene, OR 97401.

Wipf & Stock
An Imprint of Wipf and Stock Publishers
199 W. 8th Ave., Suite 3
Eugene, OR 97401

www.wipfandstock.com

PAPERBACK ISBN: 979-8-3852-4079-1
HARDCOVER ISBN: 979-8-3852-4080-7
EBOOK ISBN: 979-8-3852-4081-4

Unless otherwise noted, all Scripture citations are from *The New King James Version* (Nashville: Thomas Nelson, 1982).

CONTENTS

The Series	9
Introduction	11
1. The Essence of Church Planting	13
Questions	21
Scriptures	23
Additional Resources	25
2. Shallow Roots and Deep Roots	27
Questions	33
Scriptures	35
Additional Resources	37
3. The Biblical Basis for Church Planting	39
Questions	45
Scriptures	47
Additional Resources	49
4. The Portrait of the Church Planter	51
Questions	69
Scriptures	71
Additional ResourcesBauckham, Richard. Bible and Mission: Christian Witness in a Postmodern World. Grand Rapids: Baker Academic, 2004.	73
5. The Portrait of the Church Planter	75
Questions	89
Scriptures	91
Additional Resources	93
6. The Portrait of the Church Planter	95
Questions	105
Scriptures	107
Additional Resources	109
7. The Portrait of the Church Planter	111
Questions	127
Scriptures	129

Additional Resources	131
8. Church Planting Strategies	133
Questions	141
Scriptures	143
Additional Resources	145
9. Preparing the Church Planting Plan	147
Questions	157
Scriptures	159
Additional Resources	161
10. Miscellaneous Concerns	163
Class Project	169
Questions	175
Scriptures	177
Additional Resources	179
Notes	181
Bibliography	185
Appendices	199
Appendix 1	201
Appendix 2	209
Appendix 3	215
Appendix 4	221
Appendix 5	227
Appendix 6	235
Appendix 7	241
Appendix 8	251
Acknowledgments	273
About the Author	277
By the Author	279
Index	283
Scripture Index	285

To the glory of God, the advancement of the Great Commission of Jesus Christ, and always to Mae, my wife and companion, in the ministerial service of the lost, the broken, and the unconcerned.

St. Paul did not gather congregations; he planted churches and did not leave a church until it was fully equipped with orders of ministry, sacraments, and tradition.

— The Reverend Roland Allen
Missionary Methods: God's Plan for Missions According to Paul.
Aneko Press, 2017.

THE SERIES

This book is part of the *Christian Vocation in Context: The D. James Kennedy Institute of Reformed Leadership Series.*

The D. James Kennedy Institute of Reformed Leadership ("the Institute") is honored to partner with Wipf and Stock Publishers to produce a collection that addresses the vocation of the Christian shepherd—the pastor—within the challenges of a secular age (Charles Taylor, *A Secular Age*, 2009). This series engages critical issues confronting the Gospel and Christian living and, thereby, pastoral ministry tasked with shepherding souls through the complexities of contemporary culture. Additionally, we aim to explore essential aspects of pastoral vocation, including calling, preparation, and ministry practice, grounded in a biblical and theological framework.

The D. James Kennedy Institute of Reformed Leadership is a ministry group within Faith for Living, Inc., a North Carolina-based 501(c)(3) nonprofit organization. Guided by our motto —to shepherd the shepherds who will shepherd the flock—we seek to honor the legacy of our namesake, The Reverend Dr.

Dennis James Kennedy (1930-2007), whose commitment to biblically faithful ministry inspires us to contend for the faith, regardless of the cultural context.

To God alone be all glory and honor.

INTRODUCTION

This book was compiled for instructional purposes and is structured like a seminary syllabus. I hope and pray that the expository truths mined from the Pastoral Epistles, some with brief commentary, will aid pastors, church planting teams, Bible study groups, and others contemplating or praying about church planting, revitalization, or pastoral ministry. Though *Deep Roots* is focused on church planting, its emphasis on biblical concepts and scriptural guidelines for gospel ministry makes it applicable to various ministry settings.

This book includes prayers, questions for reflection, and biblical commentary. It is not a "how-to" manual. Practical guides, case studies, and research are invaluable and certainly have their place in a well-rounded syllabus for church planting. However, this work is not intended as a critique or protest against other approaches but rather as an affirmation. *Deep Roots* aims to supplement the growing body of insights into this crucial apostolic work of church extension by exploring divine instructions for God's mission and the Church's vocation.

Ultimately, I hope this book goes beyond instruction. *Deep Roots* seeks to inspire reflection on "who we must become" rather than "what we must do." In this sense, it is a humble appeal to approach church planting, revitalization, or any mission as a spiritual discipline to be cultivated. Our vocation is also our sanctification. May you know the joy of God as you dig into the soil of human souls. May your studies in church planting lead to the salvation of many as you plant the seeds of everlasting life in those you encounter.

Even now, I pray for the one reading these words. May the Spirit of the living God move across time and distance, thought, and physical media to unite our hearts in advancing the gospel of our God and Savior, Jesus Christ.

Michael Anthony Milton
The Twenty-first Sunday after Pentecost, 2024
Tryon, North Carolina

1

THE ESSENCE OF CHURCH PLANTING

"I planted, Apollos watered, but God gave the growth" (1 Corinthians 3:6 ESV).

Church planting is nothing more and nothing less than a believer's obedient response to Jesus Christ's Great Commission. Specifically, it is the faithful undertaking of a pastoral leader within the Christian community, burdened by God's call, to bring the light of the Gospel to a people in need. This divine burden drives the vision of church planting: to lift the weight of sin, to disciple, and to bring transformation through Christ.

We are charged with God's mission to make disciples, baptize, and teach them to observe all that Jesus commanded (Matthew 28:19-20). While many methods may address individual aspects of this mission, only one encompasses its fullness—establishing and sustaining local churches, or "Golden Lampstands," as referred to in Scripture. These churches, under Christ's reign, mediated through His ordained ministers, are the means God has chosen for transgenerational discipleship. Church planting and the ongoing life of the local church is not merely one way of responding to the Great Commission; it is God's full expression of it. It is His ordained plan for the ages.

To fulfill the Great Commission fully, we must recognize that it requires more than itinerant preaching or personal evangelism. While these are essential components of the work, they do not encompass the totality of what Christ commands. To baptize, one must acknowledge that this sacrament implies the presence of ordained ministry and a covenant community into which the new believer is enfolded. Likewise, teaching "all that Christ has commanded" is not a task completed in a single encounter but is undertaken within the context of a community that gathers faithfully around Word and Sacrament, nurtured by the church's ongoing ministry.

Some may object, citing alternative methods—monastic orders, house churches, or Bible studies. While each has its place in the broader Christian tradition, they lack the fullness of the apostolic model. In Titus 1:5, Paul instructs Titus to appoint elders in every city, unmistakably calling for structured, apostolic order within the local church. Informal gatherings of believers, while beneficial, do not fulfill the Great Commission completely unless they evolve into ordered ministries of Word and Sacrament. Without this apostolic oversight, the task remains incomplete.

Establishing these "Golden Lampstands," local churches, is the heart of church planting. The individual called to this task is not merely a preacher but a church planter—a man gifted, burdened, called, and sent by God to establish these churches.

THE CHURCH PLANTER: GIFTED, BURDENED, AND CALLED

The church planter is not just a preacher or evangelist; he is a unique figure, called like the apostles to lay foundations where none exist. Like Paul, he builds on no other man's foundation (Romans 15:20). His spiritual gifts are shaped by his education, life experiences, and passions. His very life is woven into the call.

This internal fire, much like the one that consumed Jeremiah, drives him to proclaim the Gospel to those who have not heard (Jeremiah 20:9). He is not content with reaching individuals alone—his vision encompasses families, communities, and even nations. His burden transcends the individual; he is called to transform the world in which the individual lives.

Like a prophet, he is often misunderstood and even mocked. Where others see only brokenness, the church planter envisions redemption unfolding. He sees communities ravaged by sin and envisions them restored through the power of Christ. His tears flow for what others find amusing, and his relentless pursuit of God's vision often makes him appear foolish to the world.

As this burden grows, it becomes a calling. As others observe his passion and dedication, internal and external confirmations emerge. His wife, peers, and church leaders witness the holy fire within him, and like the church in Antioch, they confirm, "This seems good to us and to the Holy Spirit" (Acts 15:28). This man is then sent forth by the church —not alone, but with the authority and support of the Body of Christ.

Is God Calling You to Church Planting? Two Questions That Can Lead to the Voice of God

Where is the source of the "voice" calling you to church planting?

For some, the "Macedonian call" to plant a church is much like a call to serve an already-formed Christian community. But the call to church planting is distinct, bearing the weight of apostolic responsibility. At least two vital elements serve as signposts on the path toward church planting. These elements do not replace the necessary assessments of gifts and graces but act as markers pointing to God's will, as described in Ephesians 2:20, and ultimately leading to that beautiful picture of *ha eretz*—the land—that Luke paints in Acts:

"So there was much joy in that city" (Acts 8:8).

I have often shared with my students and younger Christian shepherds that these two questions are critical to discerning whether God is leading them toward the extraordinary ministry of planting a church.

1. To be called to church planting is to be called to a place.

The burden for ministry—what we might call "God's burden for His people"—must resonate deeply as you consider a particular city, suburban village, or rural stretch of land. You do not simply visit a core group and visualize a congregation forming. Instead, you must look beyond these individuals, often remnants of an existing Christian presence, and catch a glimpse of a larger, unformed community. These are not perfect representatives but faithful souls that God uses to point you toward a "burning city." The vision is not simply of this initial group; it is of a people yet unseen.

The call to a place begins with a burden for the brokenness in that community. That brokenness might be poverty, injustice, wickedness, unbelief, confusion, or the entrenchment of false teachings. It may even be the spiritual lethargy that has left the secular world of the West in Satan's ready grasp—where minions scarcely need to lift a finger. This awareness of brokenness brings a burden, and the burden is what begins to shape the vision of the church plant. The vision is the thing that lifts the burden and brings Gospel wholeness to the wound you've observed. It is never simply a clever slogan for a church campaign. It is the holy foresight that sees healing coming to spiritual (and sometimes physical) wounds.

There is a sacred, unseen cord that binds the burden and the vision together. As you contemplate church planting, you should search for this dynamic—not merely within a core group—but in a broader community context, where a more extraordinary story is unfolding.

2. To be called to church planting is to embrace the "already and not yet."[1]

Borrowing from George Eldon Ladd's eschatology, this phrase describes the sacred vocation calling you to be a faithful presence of Jesus Christ in this place for the next generation. An internal voice whispers, "Will there be a Christian witness here? Will there be a community of word, sacrament, and prayer?" And further, "Will this Christian community have a biblical and theological foundation strong enough to endure until Christ returns?" The vision you are called to see is of a "Golden Lampstand" being planted in the soil of this place—a beacon for the light of Christ to shine.

There will be both internal and external evidence to support this vision. I often say that a church planter is on fire for the Gospel, burning so brightly that others come to watch him burn—and eventually get caught up in the flame. The church planter becomes the "burning man" and the "believing man." He stands with another on the edge of a vacant lot amidst the decay of urban blight or perhaps on a pristine suburban lawn concealing spiritual wounds and points out to a faraway place. "Do you see the church there?" The person looks but sees nothing.

"No, Pastor, there's only a vacant field."

"Ah, my friend, look with eyes of faith. I see your great-grandchildren worshiping here! I see what is missing now because the Church has filled this place with the presence of Christ."

At first, the listener doesn't see it. But soon, with some squinting of the soul, the vision begins to form. The pastor has kindled belief in the heart of another. That's the "already and not yet" reality of the church planter's calling.

Though not exhaustive, these two questions touch on matters of the Spirit often neglected in pragmatic conversations about church planting. And yet, isn't the work of ministry first and always a spiritual endeavor?

Ultimately, the response to these questions is a response to the mission heart of Jesus. When the prospective church planter hears both the question and the answer rising within, he hears the only voice that truly matters: the voice of the Spirit of God leading His servants to proclaim the unsearchable riches of Christ.

And because of those faithful shepherds, there will be multitudes safe in the arms of Jesus (1 Thessalonians 2:19-20).

THE WORK OF THE CHURCH PLANTER

Once called and sent, the church planter stands amid a community, proclaiming the coming of God's Kingdom. He is a preacher, but more than that—he is a herald of God's reign, establishing a local congregation that will live out God's purposes until Christ returns.

He is not a businessman starting a franchise; he is a servant of God, empowered by the Spirit, who understands that the church is a living organism, growing and advancing like yeast through the dough (Matthew 13:33). His work is spiritual, driven by the Word of God, and sustained by the Holy Spirit. He preaches the Gospel with power, trusting that Christ will build His church through this proclamation.

Like Moses, he stands before the people, proclaiming the promises of God. Like Paul, he labors day and night to build up the saints. And like John the Baptist, he prepares the way for the coming of the Lord. The church planter's work is not finished when a church is established. Instead, it only begins as he seeks to set in order the things that remain (Titus 1:5). A local government under the Lordship of Christ is put in place, elders are appointed, and the congregation begins its ministry.

CONCLUSION

Church planting is no mere project or program; it is the highest expression of the Great Commission. God's purposes are fulfilled through the local church, souls are saved, and generations are discipled. Communities are healed, and the glory of God is revealed. This is the essence of church planting, and this is the call of the church planter.

Prayer

Lord of the Harvest, You who have called us to labor in Your field, teach us to rely on Your strength and seek Your glory in all we do. May we be faithful in planting, watering, and trusting You alone to bring the growth that endures. In Jesus' name, Amen.

QUESTIONS
FOR DISCUSSION AND REFLECTION

FOR CHAPTER ONE

1. How does the local church serve as the fullest expression of the Great Commission?
2. In what ways does church planting differ from other forms of evangelism or ministry?
3. Reflect on the role of the church planter as described in this chapter. How is his burden both internal and external?
4. Why is establishing a local church so critical to fulfilling the commands of Jesus in Matthew 28:19-20?
5. Discuss the importance of apostolic order and ordained ministry in the church's life. How does this shape our understanding of church planting?
6. How can the church planter balance his visionary calling with the practical needs of establishing and sustaining a local congregation?

SCRIPTURES
FOR MEDITATION AND MEMORIZATION

- "For if I preach the gospel, that gives me no ground for boasting. For necessity is laid upon me. Woe to me if I do not preach the gospel!" (1 Corinthians 9:16 ESV)
- "For I am not ashamed of the gospel, for it is the power of God for salvation to everyone who believes, to the Jew first and also to the Greek. For in it the righteousness of God is revealed from faith for faith, as it is written, 'The righteous shall live by faith.'" (Romans 1:16-17 ESV)
- "For we cannot but speak the things which we have seen and heard." (Acts 4:20 NKJV)
- "Go, for he is a chosen vessel of Mine to bear My name before Gentiles, kings, and the children of Israel." (Acts 9:15 NKJV)

―――

ADDITIONAL RESOURCES

1. Chester, Tim. *Multiplying Churches: Reaching Today's Communities through Church Planting.* Bletchley: Authentic Media, 2006.
2. Milton, Michael A. "A Burden for Revival."
3. Murray, Stuart. *Church Planting: Laying Foundations.* Scottdale: Herald Press, 2001.
4. Yates, Richard Hibbert. "The Place of Church Planting in Mission: Towards a Theological Framework." *Evangelical Review of Theology* 33 (2009): 316–331.
5. Hutton, Trevor. *Rooting the Practice of Evangelical Protestant Church Planting within a Trinitarian Theological Framework.* PhD diss., University of Manchester, 2018.

2
SHALLOW ROOTS AND DEEP ROOTS

"Blessed is the man who walks not in the counsel of the wicked, nor stands in the way of sinners, nor sits in the seat of scoffers; but his delight is in the law of the Lord, and on his law he meditates day and night" (Psalm 1:1-2 ESV).

I once planted a young dogwood tree, but it withered and died despite my care. Consulting a horticulturist, I discovered the issue was shallow roots—the roots remained too close to the surface, unable to access the essential nutrients required during times of stress. The lesson was simple yet profound: without deep roots, no care would help the tree thrive.

Much like that dogwood, the church requires deep roots to withstand the trials of ministry and life. As individual believers grow in the grace and knowledge of God (2 Peter 3:18), so must churches establish themselves in the deep soil of biblical truth. A church with shallow roots may sprout quickly but falter under adversity, unable to draw the spiritual nourishment needed to endure. This lesson is particularly vital for church planters, who must focus on growth and prioritize depth. A church rooted deeply in Scripture will flourish across generations, standing as a "Golden Lampstand" for the glory of Christ.

THE EXAMPLE OF MOSES

Consider Moses. In his early attempt to fulfill God's burden for Israel, he acted in his own strength, slaying an Egyptian in a misguided effort to deliver his people. This failure reflects the shallow church planter who leans on worldly methods—charisma, cultural trends, or organizational strategies—rather than on God's vision and power. Only in the wilderness did Moses learn obedience and dependence on God, receiving his true calling in the encounter at the burning bush (Exodus 3:1-10).

In that moment, Moses' mission became clear, providing a powerful metaphor for the church planter's call to build deeply rooted churches. Just as Moses learned to rely on God's presence and power, so must we in planting churches that will endure. But what, then, are the marks of a shallow-rooted church, and how do we recognize them?

DIAGNOSING SHALLOW-ROOTED CHURCHES

1 A Shallow Church Is Built on a Vision Other Than God's

Moses' initial vision for Israel's freedom was his own, driven by a human impulse to act. It wasn't until he encountered God in the burning bush that he received a divine vision. Likewise, a church founded on human ideas or ambition rather than God's revelation will lack the depth required to withstand the inevitable trials of ministry. A church planter's vision must be rooted in the timeless truth of God's Word, or it will prove insufficient (Proverbs 19:21).

2 A Shallow Church Lacks a Foundation of Prayer

Just as Moses' calling began with a conversation with God, so must every church planting endeavor be birthed in prayer. Churches planted without prayer may seem well-organized, but they lack the spiritual depth of constant communion with God. Even the best strategies are shallow without prayer as a foundation (Philippians 4:6-7).

3 A Shallow Church Is Led by Someone Without a Divine Call

Moses did not initiate his mission; God called him. Similarly, a church planter must have an inward sense of calling that the outward witness of the Church confirms. Without a clear divine call, a church will lack the spiritual authority and direction necessary to make a lasting impact. This calling, validated by the local church, is a fundamental root of deep ministry (Romans 10:15; Acts 13:2-3).

4 A Shallow Church Is Based on Anecdotes, Not Theology

Moses encountered the living God, not a set of techniques or anecdotes. Shallow churches are often built on popular trends or inspirational stories, while deep-rooted churches are grounded in the unchanging truths of Scripture and sound doctrine. Theology provides the deep roots that enable a church to withstand cultural and spiritual storms (2 Timothy 4:2-4).

5 A Shallow Church Is Not Driven by a Burden for Others

God saw the suffering of His people and sent Moses to deliver them. A deep-rooted church is burdened with the community's spiritual and physical needs, serving as a transformative presence. Without reducing the mission to social causes, a church with deep roots brings Christ's love to bear on all of life's challenges, embodying the compassion of the Good Shepherd (Matthew 9:36; John 10:11).

6 A Shallow Church Neglects the Ultimate Goal: The Salvation of Souls

Moses was sent to deliver Israel from bondage and lead them to the Promised Land. Likewise, the church's central mission is to proclaim the Gospel, leading souls to salvation in Christ and nurturing them in faith. A church rooted deeply in this purpose will prioritize eternal outcomes over temporary gains, ensuring that its ministry is grounded in the salvation of souls and the glory of God (Matthew 28:19-20; John 17:3).

CONCLUSION

The image of the tree in Psalm 1 beautifully illustrates the essence of a deeply rooted church: *"He is like a tree planted by streams of water that yields its fruit in its season, and its leaf does not wither"* (Psalm 1:3 ESV). A church that delights in God's Word, is sustained by prayer, and is strengthened by the Holy Spirit stands firm, bearing fruit for future generations. It does not shrink in times of trial but is a living testament to God's sustaining power.

PRAYER

Almighty and most merciful Father,
　Whose love is boundless and beyond human understanding, manifested so wondrously in the gift of Thine only-begotten Son, our Savior, Jesus Christ,

Grant that we, who seek to fulfill the Great Commission through the planting of churches rooted in Thy Holy Word and burdened for the souls of men,

May ever delight in the contemplation of Thy unsearchable love and radiant majesty.

As we preach or pray, sing or sit in silence, labor or rest,
May we be immersed in the depths of Thy truth,
that with hearts and minds enlarged,
We may trust wholly in Thy Word to accomplish in others what it has wrought in us.

Thus may we lay firm and unshakable foundations
for a spiritual house to the praise and glory of Thy Name,
through the mighty working of Thy Spirit,
for the eternal good of Thy people,
and the coming of Thy kingdom,
wherein shall dwell righteousness,
in the new heavens and the new earth.
Amen.

QUESTIONS
FOR REFLECTION AND DISCUSSION

FOR CHAPTER TWO

1. How does understanding a supernatural call to ministry impact a church planting or revitalization effort?
2. What do you see as the main hindrance in church planting teams, e.g., recognizing the supernatural activity of Jesus building His Church through our work?
3. How do shallow roots affect the Kingdom of God in a given community?
4. How do deep-rooted churches become shallow?
5. How do shallow roots become deep?

SCRIPTURES
FOR MEDITATION AND MEMORIZATION

- "Let Your work be shown to Your servants, and Your glorious power to their children. Let the favor of the Lord our God be upon us, and establish the work of our hands upon us; yes, establish the work of our hands!" (Psalm 90:16-17 ESV)
- "Even if you have ten thousand guardians in Christ, you do not have many fathers; for in Christ Jesus I became your father through the gospel." (1 Corinthians 4:15 NIV)
- "If others share this rightful claim on you, do not we even more? Nevertheless, we have not made use of this right, but we endure anything rather than put an obstacle in the way of the gospel of Christ." (1 Corinthians 9:12 ESV)
- "In the same way, the Lord commanded that those who proclaim the gospel should get their living by the gospel." (1 Corinthians 9:14 ESV)

———

ADDITIONAL RESOURCES

1. DeYoung, Kevin, and Greg Gilbert. *What Is the Mission of the Church? Making Sense of Social Justice, Shalom, and the Great Commission.* Wheaton, IL: Crossway, 2011.
2. Helm, David R. *Expositional Preaching: How We Speak God's Word Today.* Wheaton, IL: Crossway, 2014.
3. Horton, Michael. *The Gospel Commission: Recovering God's Strategy for Making Disciples.* Grand Rapids: Baker Books, 2011.
4. Milton, Michael A. "The Blessings of Revival." YouTube video, accessed [insert access date]. https://youtu.be/jOnvPfYEiAo.
5. Stott, John. *The Living Church: Convictions of a Lifelong Pastor.* Downers Grove, IL: IVP Books, 2007.
6. Clowney, Edmund P. *The Church.* Downers Grove, IL: IVP Academic, 1995.

3
THE BIBLICAL BASIS FOR CHURCH PLANTING

"It is too light a thing that you should be my servant to raise up the tribes of Jacob and to bring back the preserved of Israel; I will make you as a light for the nations, that my salvation may reach to the end of the earth" (Isaiah 49:6 ESV).

THE BIBLICAL BASIS FOR CHURCH PLANTING

The Biblical basis for church planting is woven throughout Scripture, from the Old Testament to the New. It is evident in the promises made to Abraham, the prophecies of renewal in Isaiah, and the Great Commission given by Jesus Christ. Church planting is the clearest fulfillment of the Gospel mandate to "make disciples of all nations" (Matthew 28:19). It establishes long-term communities of faith where the Word of God is preached, the sacraments are administered, and believers are disciples.

OLD TESTAMENT FOUNDATIONS

The Old Testament lays the groundwork for the expansive nature of God's plan of salvation. While it is true that God chose Israel as His peculiar people, it was never His intention for the covenant to remain with them alone. The promises made to Abraham included that "all peoples on earth will be blessed through you" (Genesis 12:3), showing that God's salvation would eventually extend to all nations. This promise is echoed throughout the Old Testament, even in the Law (Deuteronomy 4:6-8), where Israel was meant to be a beacon of God's wisdom to the nations.

Isaiah 49:6 clarifies: "I will make you a light for the nations, that my salvation may reach the end of the earth." Here, God's vision for salvation was always centrifugal, spinning outward to embrace the world. As God's servant, Jesus Christ came not only to restore Israel but to be the Savior of the whole world (John 1:29). The Old Testament provides the foundation for understanding that church planting is not a new idea but a continuation of God's unfolding plan to bring redemption to all creation.

JUST US AND NO MORE

Unfortunately, there are times when both individuals and congregations fall into a "just us and no more" mindset, closing themselves off to the work of evangelism and church planting. Some even argue that the Old Testament lacks a theology of mission. But this is a misunderstanding of the Old Testament's witness. From Isaiah to the Psalms, the Old Testament prophets speak of a future in which the nations come to know and worship the Lord. Psalm 67, for example, declares,

"May the peoples praise you, God; may all the peoples praise you" (Psalm 67:3).

The story of Israel is not one of exclusivity but of God's unfolding plan to redeem all of creation. God's covenant with Abraham set the stage for the inclusion of all nations, and Isaiah's prophecy confirms that Israel was meant to be a light to the Gentiles. The natural outworking of this light-bearing mission is planting churches—communities of faith that proclaim Christ's lordship and extend the invitation to enter the Kingdom.

THE EXPANSIVE NATURE OF GOD'S SALVATION

Isaiah 49:6 reveals that it is "too small" a thing for God's servant to focus only on Israel. God's salvation is expansive, encompassing the Gentiles and the "ends of the earth" (Acts 1:8). This demonstrates that church planting is not a modern innovation but a natural extension of God's redemptive plan throughout history. The Gospel, by its very nature, is meant to spread.

Churches must not become inwardly focused but must continually look outward to the nations, fulfilling the Great Commission. As the prophet Habakkuk declares, "For the earth will be filled with the knowledge of the glory of the Lord as the waters cover the sea" (Habakkuk 2:14). The church planter's work is grounded in this expansive vision of God's kingdom.

NEW TESTAMENT CONTINUATION

The New Testament further amplifies this theme. Jesus' ministry was focused mainly on the "lost sheep of Israel" (Matthew 15:24), but after His resurrection, the scope of the mission expanded dramatically. In Matthew 28:19-20, Jesus commissions His disciples, saying, "Go therefore and make disciples of all nations, baptizing them in the name of the Father and the Son and the Holy Spirit, teaching them to observe all that I have commanded you." This command clarifies that the church's mission is outward-focused, and planting new churches is how this mission is fulfilled.

The apostles, empowered by the Holy Spirit at Pentecost (Acts 2), were sent to make disciples, baptize, and teach. This led to the establishment of churches wherever they went. Paul's ministry is a prime example. He did not merely evangelize; he planted churches that would continue to grow and spread the Gospel long after he moved on (Acts 14:23). His letters were primarily addressed to churches or individuals involved in leading churches, showing that establishing new congregations was central to the early Christian mission (e.g., 1 Corinthians, Galatians, Ephesians).

THE LIGHTHOUSE PARABLE

The image of the lighthouse, initially established to rescue shipwrecked sailors but later becoming a museum of past glories, serves as a warning to churches today. Church planting is not about building monuments to the past but about continually reaching out to the lost with the light of Christ. Jesus warns of this in His parable of the talents (Matthew 25:14-30), where the servant who buries his talent is condemned for failing to invest in the future.

A healthy, deep-rooted church will always be outward-looking, committed to planting new churches to extend the reach of the Gospel. As Jesus said in Matthew 5:14-16, "You are the light of the world. A town built on a hill cannot be hidden." The work of church planting ensures that this light continues to shine, generation after generation.

CONCLUSION

The Biblical basis for church planting is clear. From the promises made to Abraham, through the prophecies of Isaiah, to the Great Commission given by Christ, God's plan has always been to redeem the world through His chosen people. Church planting is the ordinary means of carrying out this redemptive mission. The church is not merely a static institution but a living, growing organism that must continually extend its reach to the ends of the earth (Isaiah 2:2-3; Acts 13:47).

———

PRAYER

O Lord God,
    whose mercy and grace are beyond measure,
    Thou didst send Thine only-begotten Son,
    our Savior, Jesus Christ,
    to deliver us from the bondage of sin
    and from the deep darkness that covered the earth.
    Yet, in the fullness of time,
    Christ pierced the darkness
    with the light of His very Person,
    the truth of His Gospel,
    and the glory of His ascendant radiance.
    By Thy Spirit, the Apostles, and the saints of old,
    proclaimed the Good News of freedom from Satan's hold,
    and Thy Gospel spread to the ends of the earth.
    Grant, we beseech Thee, that in our day,
    we may know Thy love,

be filled with Thy power,
and have the vision of the New Heaven and the New Earth
engraved upon the eyes of our souls.
So may we, too,
go forth and tell of the marvelous works
which Thou hast wrought in Christ Jesus our Lord,
who liveth and reigneth with Thee, O Father,
and the Holy Ghost,
one God, world without end.
Amen.

QUESTIONS
FOR REFLECTION AND DISCUSSION

FOR CHAPTER THREE

1. How does the Old Testament lay a foundation for the church's mission to the nations?
2. In what ways does Isaiah 49:6 shape our understanding of the scope of God's redemptive plan?
3. Why is church planting essential for fulfilling the Great Commission, as seen in the New Testament?
4. How can churches avoid becoming inwardly focused and losing their missional vision?
5. What lessons can we learn from Paul's church-planting strategy that can be applied today?
6. How does the parable of the Lighthouse illustrate the importance of remaining faithful to the church's mission of reaching the lost?

SCRIPTURES
FOR MEDITATION AND MEMORIZATION

- "Now when I went to Troas to preach the gospel of Christ, even though a door was opened for me in the Lord..." (2 Corinthians 2:12 ESV)
- "And I also say to you that you are Peter, and on this rock I will build My church, and the gates of Hades shall not prevail against it." (Matthew 16:18 NKJV)
- "After this I looked, and behold, a great multitude that no one could number, from every nation, from all tribes and peoples and languages, standing before the throne and before the Lamb, clothed in white robes, with palm branches in their hands..." (Revelation 7:9 ESV)
- "And Jesus came and spoke to them, saying, 'All authority has been given to Me in heaven and on earth. Go therefore and make disciples of all the nations, baptizing them in the name of the Father and of the Son and of the Holy Spirit, teaching them to observe all things that I have commanded you;

and lo, I am with you always, even to the end of the age.'" (Matthew 28:18-20 NKJV)

ADDITIONAL RESOURCES

1. Allen, Roland. *Missionary Methods: St. Paul's or Ours?* Grand Rapids: Eerdmans, 1962.
2. DeYoung, Kevin. *What Is the Mission of the Church?* Wheaton, IL: Crossway, 2011.
3. Hesselgrave, David J. *Planting Churches Cross-Culturally: North America and Beyond.* Grand Rapids: Baker Books, 2000.
4. Murray, Iain H. *The Puritan Hope: Revival and the Interpretation of Prophecy.* Edinburgh: Banner of Truth, 1971.
5. Piper, John. *Let the Nations Be Glad! The Supremacy of God in Missions.* Grand Rapids: Baker Academic, 2003.
6. Stott, John. *The Living Church: Convictions of a Lifelong Pastor.* Downers Grove, IL: IVP Books, 2007.

4
THE PORTRAIT OF THE CHURCH PLANTER
PART ONE

"I myself will be the shepherd of my sheep, and I myself will make them lie down, declares the Lord God. I will seek the lost, and I will bring back the strayed, and I will bind up the injured, and I will strengthen the weak, and the fat and the strong I will destroy. I will feed them in justice" (Ezekiel 34:15-16 ESV).

The Life, Faith, and Ministry of the Church Planter in 1 and 2 Timothy

Church planting calls for a specific set of traits that distinguish it from other pastoral roles (each expression of pastoral ministry carries unique characteristics suited to its purpose). This chapter highlights essential characteristics of the church planter as drawn from Paul's letters to Timothy. Though these qualities apply broadly to all pastors, they are particularly crucial for those called to the formidable work of establishing new congregations. At their core, church planters are men called by God and set apart for this sacred task—

entrusted with gathering, nurturing, and shepherding nascent communities through the divinely appointed means of grace: Word, Sacrament, and Prayer.

Assessment and Calling

A lack of careful assessment—character and doctrine, gifts and limitations, burden and vision, and practical issues that could either enhance or hinder the mission—often lies in the ruins of failed church plants. Before sending a church planter to the field, it is essential to evaluate his calling, gifts, and spiritual readiness thoroughly. This chapter will seek to discover and express what Scripture reveals about the foundational qualities necessary in a church planter, with a particular focus on 1 and 2 Timothy. Paul's pastoral letters remind us that church leaders should look beyond surface traits to discern a God-given burden in the planter's heart—a calling for a specific people or place that aligns with the purposes of God. This sacred burden, paired with character and calling, becomes a guiding force for faithful ministry (1 Timothy 3:1-7; 2 Timothy 4:2).

The Apostle Paul himself serves as an example. Though appointed as the Apostle to the Gentiles (Galatians 2:7-8), Paul carried a profound love for his fellow Hebrews, preaching to them in Jerusalem and engaging with Jewish communities in synagogues across Asia Minor and Europe (Romans 9:1-3; Acts 13:5; 14:1). Yet, his unambiguous mission—to bring the Gospel to the Gentiles—was given directly by the risen Christ (Acts 9:15-16). Every other ministry flowed to or from this singular, divinely appointed passion (Philippians 3:13-14).

With this foundation, we begin our study in 1 Timothy. Paul, with apostolic authority, sent one man to one church and another elsewhere. Though often reserved about his authority, it is never in doubt. We remember that while the office of *apostle*—those with a personal call from Christ—is now complete, the role of the evangelist continues. This office holds a kind of apostolic-like authority in superintending the work of establishing orderly Christian communities with proper, godly oversight and representation of the catholic faith—the apostolic faith common to the men whom Christ directly called: *"For this reason I left you in Crete, that you should set in order the things that are lacking, and appoint elders in every city as I commanded you—"* (Titus 1:5). The Reformers later exercised the office of evangelist within their own national ministries, at times progressing into pastoral ministry (as with Calvin) or maintaining an evangelical oversight (as with Luther and Knox).

The Pastoral Epistles—1 and 2 Timothy and Titus—are thus written to those whom Paul has commissioned and who have taken up this evangelical oversight. Titus was charged with the work in Crete, and Timothy with a fledgling Christian community in Ephesus. Through our study of 1 and 2 Timothy, we will examine their specific challenges and their scriptural responses to each. Like a proto-Rembrandt, Constable, or Turner, Paul combines shadow and light with profound artistic and intellectual abilities—strokes of strengths and vulnerabilities, with insights for threats and opportunities—to paint a masterly portrait of the church planter. It is, thus, a portrait gallery inspired by the Holy Spirit for our instruction. Our work is to observe and convey these characteristics, which remain essential for the Church's mission today.

> "A true shepherd knows no calling higher than to lead his flock into the green pastures of Christ, and to guard them against the wolves that seek to scatter." — Charles Haddon Spurgeon.[1]

PORTRAIT OF A CHURCH PLANTER

1. A Man Called by God and Who Knows It

Paul opens with a decisive affirmation of his divine calling: *"Paul, an apostle of Christ Jesus by command of God"* (1 Timothy 1:1). Similarly, a church planter must be assured of his calling—not merely sensing it within himself but also having that call confirmed by others in the church. It is not simply advisable but essential that both clerical and lay representatives within the Christian assembly examine a man for the work of a pastor or evangelist. Equally, the one presenting himself for this work must do so only after exhaustive biblical introspection, discernment, and prayerful consideration. This process should include if married, his wife, and if single, parents, siblings, or close friends who represent the Church in an informal but equally intentional way.

2. A Man Who Invests in Other Church Planters

Church planting is not solitary. The planter must invest in the next generation of leaders, as Paul did with Timothy: "To Timothy, my true child in the faith" (1 Timothy 1:2). This introduction might be glossed over, and one moves to the meat of the message. In doing so, however, one would miss an enormously important truth and guide to the rest of the epistle.

Paul will write to Timothy so that every sentence is filled with choice words that give instructions through modeling. The old saying writing by "showing, not telling" is in view here. Paul addresses Timothy as his true child in the faith." This is not only a term of endearment but a testimony to how God brought these men together. The memory of those affectionate bonds and the recognition of the providence of the Lord at work in his life will bring both assurance and hope to Pastor Timothy. Moreover, he must ask himself, "Am I making disciples of Christ here in such a way as I am also mentoring another generation of Christian shepherds?"

From day one, the church planter—in his office as an evangelist—must be asking God to guide him to young men who may be challenged with the call to ministry and, where appropriate, to begin passing along the apostolic faith and the work of shepherding.

3. A Decisive Man

The church planter must act decisively in his leadership: "As I urged you" (1 Timothy 1:3). A strong sense of direction and purpose is essential to guide a fledgling congregation. Like all other virtues and characteristics needed, decisiveness (thoughtful evaluation, reviewed with Biblical faithfulness, and applied to the goal of evangelism and discipleship, or, we might say, "Christian critical thinking") is a logical consequence of a living vocation. The continuous internal spiritual fission— the burden igniting the values and causing a reaction that produces vision and mission—creates the virtues and graces necessary to gather a covenanted Christian community.

4. A Man Called to a Specific Place

Paul's instruction to Timothy to remain in Ephesus (1 Timothy 1:3) underscores that church planting involves both establishing a new congregation and remaining to nurture its growth over time. This directive raises a crucial question for those called as evangelists: *Is my goal to establish a Christian community, spiritually and practically cultivated (Psalm 90:17)— through divine anointing and labor—that will eventually call another shepherd?* Drawing from biblical principles and experience, I offer these reflections:

1 If you intend to establish a congregation and then pass the pastoral role to another, be clear about this from the outset.

Some will join the assembly and engage in Word, Sacrament, and Prayer, building a relationship with you as their pastor-teacher. Even when a church planter makes clear his intention to depart and eventually continue the larger mission of planting, there is a natural, emotional attachment within the congregation, which can create challenges. Disappointment and a sense of unsettledness are likely when the time for transition comes. If this expectation goes unspoken, members may assume the church planter will stay as their seated pastor, leading to considerable disillusionment when he announces plans to leave for another mission. For some, the departure may feel like a form of "betrayal," resulting in strained relationships and, potentially, an irreparable setback for the community's spiritual and organizational health.

2 If you feel called to remain with the new congregation as its pastor, do not assume this call without the church's formal affirmation.

Acting as the *de facto* pastor without an official call from the congregation risks presumption. In every circumstance, the principle of the internal call substantiated by an external call must be honored. Even if the congregation expresses enthusiasm or affection toward your continued leadership, ensure they can formally voice their corporate approbation through an official call. This approach requires pastoral care and sensitivity; it is crucial not to unsettle the congregation or create unintended fear of your departure. Similarly, it ensures that you do not overlook the potential for a surprising outcome should the congregation wish to call a different pastor. If all indications are positive and the congregation's affirmation aligns with your sense of calling, you can proceed with a formal call, solidifying your role as pastor of the church you planted.

In sum, my advice is this: *Do not presume upon the goodwill of others and do not presume upon the Holy Spirit.* As Scripture reminds us, *"The heart of man plans his way, but the Lord establishes his steps"* (Proverbs 16:9).

5. A Theologian

A church planter must be thoroughly grounded in sound doctrine. Paul urges Timothy to protect the church from false teachings, emphasizing the critical role of a church planter as a vigilant student of Scripture (1 Timothy 1:3). The responsibility to "rightly divide the word of truth" (2 Timothy 2:15) underscores the necessity of doctrinal soundness for those establishing new congregations.

While I have addressed the value of ministerial education and training elsewhere, it is worth reiterating that the Christian shepherd must be deeply versed in the knowledge of God (Proverbs 2:6) and equipped for the work of shepherding. This preparation goes beyond formal theological study, though seminary or its equivalent is invaluable. It involves an apprenticeship model that fosters both theological depth and pastoral skill, aligning with Paul's example of training Timothy through personal mentorship (2 Timothy 2:2).

Furthermore, education and training should be lifelong pursuits. Scripture encourages continuous growth in understanding: *"Let the wise hear and increase in learning, and the one who understands obtain guidance"* (Proverbs 1:5). With time in ministry comes the opportunity to read more widely and deeply, to seek counsel from others (Proverbs 11:14), and to consider the role of a Christian shepherd from various perspectives, enriching one's pastoral approach. This commitment to lifelong learning enables you to fulfill your scriptural mandate as a diligent laborer in the Word (1 Timothy 5:17) and as a spiritual physician equipped to minister to the human soul (Hebrews 4:12).

6. A Bold Preacher of Gospel Truth

A church planter *must not avoid* confronting error (1

Timothy 1:3-7). I prefer to state this in the negative rather than to suggest actively seeking out error. Paul's letters often address falsehoods and theological mistakes as they arise naturally within the church, and he exemplifies a skilled, pastoral discernment that balances necessary correction with compassion. This is a crucial, though often overlooked and sometimes mishandled, aspect of ministry that calls for both wisdom and care.

Boldness in proclaiming truth is indispensable, especially in an age where many promote deceptive doctrines (2 Timothy 4:3-4). Paul's charge to Timothy underscores the necessity of guarding the flock against false teachings and unwaveringly upholding sound doctrine (Titus 1:9).

The importance of teaching biblical truth cannot be overstated: *"You shall know the truth, and the truth shall make you free"* (John 8:32). False teachings lead to spiritual bondage, while the truths of the Gospel bring liberation. The church planter's role is to preach the Word of God faithfully, trusting that the Spirit will work through His Word—convicting, convincing, or prompting reflection in those who hear (Isaiah 55:11).

At times, the reaction to truth may be intense opposition. Jesus Himself encountered such resistance when confronting demonic powers; as He commanded a spirit to depart, it convulsed the man in its last act of defiance before yielding to Christ's authority (Mark 1:25-26). The church planter may face similar resistance, but this opposition ultimately testifies to the power of the truth.

7. A Man Who Loves People

At the heart of church planting is a deep love for people. Paul reminds Timothy that *"the aim of our charge is love"* (1 Timothy 1:5). The church planter is driven by a desire for the spiritual well-being of those in his care, understanding that effective leadership flows from genuine love: one cannot truly lead those he does not love.

The church planter's love reaches both those already gathered and the vast plains of unbelief—a boundless stretch of villages where blue-gray smoke from countless huts rises, forming a dense canopy of smog that blankets an endless sea of humanity. And so, with eyes of faith, the church planter sees beyond the immediate congregation to those countless communities around him—places where lives are lived, families gather, work is done, and souls pass into eternity. Into one of these communities, he is called to go. Why? Because he is one of them, bound by shared humanity, and yet he carries a burden for the consequences of sin, the bondage of the soul, and the sorrow it brings (Romans 9:2-3). Compelled by love, he longs for them to know the Lord Jesus, who has set him free (Galatians 5:1). If this burden for the lost among us does not disturb and compel the church planter to respond, it is not only a scandal before those who sent him but, infinitely more, a profound tragedy for those who remain unreached.

8. A Man Who Sees Himself as a Steward of the Gospel

Church planters carry a sacred trust as stewards of the Gospel, serving for the benefit of others. Paul emphasizes this responsibility, saying, *"according to the glorious gospel of the blessed God which was committed to my trust"* (1 Timothy 1:11). Paul exemplifies the stewardship that he calls Timothy to emulate, demonstrating how his life and ministry embody this commitment. Like Paul, Timothy is charged with faithfully managing the Gospel, entrusted to keep it safe and grow and advance it.

A faithful steward does not simply return the master's property; he invests and increases its value, echoing the parable of the talents where servants are called to invest wisely what was given (Matthew 25:14-30). Likewise, the church planter is entrusted with the Gospel not for preservation alone but for actively advancing God's Kingdom. This is accomplished by "making disciples of all nations" (Matthew 28:19), enfolding others into a life of following the Lord Jesus, and teaching them to observe all that He commanded (Matthew 28:20). In this way, the church planter fulfills his role as a steward, presenting the fruit of a multiplied and growing faith to the glory of God.

9. A Man Burning with the Gospel in His Own Life

Among the most critical passages in 1 Timothy for Timothy's ministry is Paul's powerful testimony of transformation by grace (1 Timothy 1:12-16):

> *"And I thank Christ Jesus our Lord who has enabled me, because He counted me faithful, putting me into the ministry, although I was formerly a blasphemer, a persecutor, and an insolent man; but I obtained mercy because I did it ignorantly in unbelief. And the grace of our Lord was exceedingly abundant, with faith and love which are in Christ Jesus. This is a faithful saying and worthy of all acceptance, that Christ Jesus came into the world to save sinners, of whom I am chief. However, for this reason I obtained mercy, that in me first Jesus Christ might show all longsuffering, as a pattern to those who are going to believe on Him for everlasting life."*

This passage is crucial because Paul demonstrates that a church planter's ministry flows directly from his personal encounter with the transforming grace of our Lord Jesus Christ. Without a life that has been touched, changed, and renewed by grace, a church planter risks becoming an empty vessel. Paul's testimony offers Timothy a vivid reminder that his ministry must be fueled by the Gospel's impact on his own life (2 Corinthians 5:17).

History gives us many sorrowful examples of ministers

who possessed the skills to preach and discern and achieved humanly impressive results, only later to reveal themselves as hypocrites or, worse, imposters. Their fall from good standing, while unable to take away genuine conversions or the growth of those who heard them and believed, nonetheless brings sorrow and dishonor that overshadows their temporary ministry success. Jesus Himself warned against those who cause harm to His flock, saying, *"It would be better for him if a millstone were hung around his neck and he were drowned in the depth of the sea"* (Matthew 18:6). Therefore, it is critical for a church planter to know Christ deeply, depend on Him entirely, and live with a reverent fear of His holiness.

A church planter should minister out of what God has done in his own life, for it is the Spirit working within him that draws others, not his own strength or charisma (Galatians 2:20). The faithful and spiritually effective church planter is an evangelist who burns with the fire of God's grace in Christ, drawing others to witness the transforming power of the Gospel. In watching this "burning man," many are drawn and transformed, joyfully consumed by the healing and renewing power of the Gospel—a continuous, life-giving reaction of *"grace upon grace"* (John 1:16) that transforms, redeems, and resurrects.

10. A Man of Worship

A church planter's heart should overflow with worship, just as Paul's does in his spontaneous doxology in 1 Timothy 1:17: *"Now to the King eternal, immortal, invisible, to God who alone is wise, be honor and glory forever and ever. Amen."* This passage reveals a profound, instructive moment as Paul's words ignite into praise, an authentic "spontaneous combustion" of worship that rises naturally from his reflection on God's work in his life.

As Paul writes about the mercy and grace he has received,

he breaks into praise, showing that worship is the inevitable response of a heart transformed by grace (Ephesians 2:4-5). One can imagine his amanuensis trying to keep pace with Paul's reasoning, only to be taken aback as Paul's logic suddenly shifts into a glorious, seemingly unplanned doxology. This overflow of praise is no rare occurrence in Paul's letters; praise and worship burst forth throughout his writings, as in Romans 11:36, where he exclaims, *"For of Him and through Him and to Him are all things, to whom be glory forever. Amen."* These moments remind Timothy—and all church planters—that the reality of the resurrection is at work in daily ministry (1 Corinthians 15:58).

Worship, then, is the natural response of a soul touched by grace and should be the heartbeat of the church planter's ministry. As Timothy leads, he is reminded that all he does must point to the glory of Christ, echoing the words of Colossians 3:17: *"And whatever you do in word or deed, do all in the name of the Lord Jesus, giving thanks to God the Father through Him."* We could indeed benefit from more of these "spontaneous combustions" of doxology in pastoral ministry as they testify to life in continual awe of God's grace, beauty, and majesty.

11. A Man Who Feels the Weight of Providence

Paul reminds Timothy that his calling was affirmed by prophetic words, underscoring the significance of recognizing God's providential hand in a church planter's calling: *"This charge I commit to you, son Timothy, according to the prophecies previously made concerning you, that by them you may wage the good warfare"* (1 Timothy 1:18). This reminder reinforces that God's guidance and purposes are central to Gospel ministry. The call to ministry—and to church planting specifically—is not a mere decision or career choice; it is a divine summons that demands a reverent and certain response. Paul's own words reflect this compulsion: *"I am compelled to preach. Woe to me if I do not preach the gospel!"* (1 Corinthians 9:16). The call to proclaim the unsearchable riches of Christ must be approached with holy resolve, acknowledging that it is God who appoints and sustains those entrusted with this mission.

I vividly recall the challenge presented by another minister at a critical time—when I was preparing to leave for seminary. We were uprooting our lives from Kansas to Fort Lauderdale so I could intern under Dr. D. James Kennedy, a move that would disrupt our family and affect my 97-year-old Aunt Eva. Her chaplain at the Lutheran care facility, a retired Nazarene minister known as "Dr. Eckley," gave me a stern but wise charge: "Mike, you must be certain of your calling from God. When you are ordained and preach the truth, and some respond with hatred, all you will have is your call. And when others speak falsely of you or your family or even try to run you out because you don't meet their preferences—*all you will have is your call.*" He continued with other examples, each underscoring the inevitable trials of ministry. Was his warning unsettling? Absolutely. But was it necessary? Experience has proven the solemn truth of his words.

Indeed, those pastoral words of wisdom stayed with me, and I delayed seminary by a year, seeking further confirmation from our local community within the Body of Christ. In time, God affirmed this call through the Church's encouragement, confirming that I was indeed set apart for the work of the Gospel (Acts 13:2-3). Looking back, I see the prudence of that challenge: when troubles come, as they inevitably do, one must know with absolute conviction that God has called them. This weight of providence is the anchor in ministry, a burden from the Spirit that compels us to preach. A hand on the shoulder

Jeremiah speaks of this holy compulsion when he says, *"His word was in my heart like a burning fire shut up in my bones; I was weary of holding it back, and I could not"* (Jeremiah 20:9). The church planter must carry this same burden—a profound sense of God's call on his life, pressing him to preach the Gospel despite any opposition. With the Spirit's weight upon his conscience, he can press forward, proclaiming truth in the certainty that he is acting under the providential hand of God.

12. A Man Fearful of Falling into Error

Paul warns Timothy of the danger of spiritual shipwreck, a vivid reminder of the need for vigilance in ministry: *"This charge I commit to you, son Timothy, according to the prophecies previously made concerning you, that by them you may wage the good warfare, having faith and a good conscience, which some having rejected, concerning the faith have suffered shipwreck, of whom are Hymenaeus and Alexander, whom I delivered to Satan that they may learn not to blaspheme"* (1 Timothy 1:18-20).

A church planter must stay close to Christ, avoiding any drift toward complacency or spiritual negligence. Scripture warns us that *"your adversary the devil prowls around like a roaring lion, seeking someone to devour"* (1 Peter 5:8). I often remind my seminary students, "Ministers are red meat to Lucifer and his demons. Church planters are red meat with salt and pepper, cooked to perfection." Church planters face a unique intensity of spiritual opposition, making them prime targets for demonic attacks. Compounding this danger are the fleshly tendencies we all wrestle with and the worldly allure of "success"—measured by numbers, fame, and other fleeting standards (Galatians 5:17; 1 John 2:16).

A close friend and fellow pastor once prayed, *"Lord, take my life before I would bring scandal upon Your name."* His prayer reflects a healthy, biblical fear of falling into error and a resolve to remain vigilant. Church planters, stay close to the cross. Live humbly before the One who bore that cross for you, and let every ministry action flow from a place of "faith and a good conscience" (1 Timothy 1:19). As Paul reminds the Corinthians, *"Let anyone who thinks that he stands take heed lest he fall"* (1 Corinthians 10:12). Our calling demands both reverence and resolve, keeping Christ at the center to guard against error and faithfully fulfill the ministry entrusted to us.

13. A Pastor Who Guides the Saints

Church planters, like pastors, are called to provide biblical guidance on matters of faith and life, even in areas that may be complex or controversial. Paul instructs Timothy on this in 1 Timothy 2:1–7:

> *"Therefore I exhort first of all that supplications, prayers, intercessions, and giving of thanks be made for all men, for kings and all who are in authority, that we may lead a quiet and peaceable life in all godliness and reverence. For this is good and acceptable in the sight of God our Savior, who desires all men to be saved and to come to the knowledge of the truth. For there is one God and one Mediator between God and men, the Man Christ Jesus, who gave Himself a ransom for all, to be testified in due time, for which I was appointed a preacher and an apostle—I am speaking the truth in Christ and not lying—a teacher of the Gentiles in faith and truth."*

Here, Paul turns Timothy's attention to public theology, specifically addressing the believer's relationship to civil authorities. He urges prayers for those in power so that Christians may live *"a quiet and peaceable life in all godliness and reverence"* (1 Timothy 2:2). Yet this peace is not sought for comfort alone; it supports God's desire that *"all men...come to the knowledge of the truth"* (v. 4). This knowledge centers on the uniqueness of Christ, the "one Mediator between God and men" (v. 5), sent as the ransom for humanity. Paul reminds Timothy—and all church planters—that praying for authorities is part of a divine mission to create a stable environment conducive to the spread of the Gospel (Romans 13:1-2).

Church planters, then, must avoid the temptation to disengage from the secular world, recognizing instead that they are called to live within it and influence it for good. As Jeremiah instructed the exiles in Babylon, *"Seek the peace of the city where I have caused you to be carried away captive, and pray to the Lord for it; for in its peace you will have peace"* (Jeremiah 29:7). Similarly, as Daniel faithfully served even those who held him captive, we, too, are to build up the communities around us, knowing that their welfare affects our own.

God has ordained that we pray for all authorities, not because the Almighty requires our prayers to accomplish His will—what role could we possibly play in the secret councils of the Triune God? Rather, He calls us to pray to draw us into a deeper relationship with Him, to cultivate a compassionate heart for the lost, and to remind us that His responses are intricately woven with the petitions of His children. This prayer is both an act of obedience and a means by which God shapes us into His likeness, aligning our hearts with His purposes.

14. A Leader Who Shares Ministry

A church planter must equip and appoint leaders, following the apostolic command and pattern given by Paul: *"And the things that you have heard from me among many witnesses, commit these to faithful men who will be able to teach others also"* (2 Timothy 2:2). Likewise, Paul instructs Titus, *"For this reason I left you in Crete, that you should set in order the things that are lacking, and appoint elders in every city as I commanded you"* (Titus 1:5).

Two essential principles emerge from this Gospel directive. Firstly, the church planter's work is not about building his own kingdom but serving as a steward in the Household of God, seeking to fulfill the Father's mission. He labors to establish a well-ordered community, a local church structured with a plurality of presbyters, both lay leaders—ruling elders and deacons—and shepherds or pastor-teachers, as exemplified in Exodus 18 and later in the synagogue structure.

Secondly, the church planter should minister with the "end in mind." This "end"—the ultimate aim of the divinely ordained project—is the ordination of elders in the Gospel community. The church planter's goal is to establish leaders who will faithfully shepherd the flock, ensuring the church's continuity and faithfulness to the mission entrusted by God.

15. A Man Who Loves the Church

Finally, the church planter must love the Church, shaping her according to the biblical patterns of faith and practice: *"so that you may know how one ought to behave in the household of God"* (1 Timothy 3:15). It is inconceivable that one could labor for God's glory in church planting without a profound, heartfelt devotion to the Body of Christ. This love is not merely for a denomination, nor solely for the history or culture of a local congregation, but for the people redeemed by God's grace, gathered into the God-ordained community where the Great Commission is fulfilled.

As James Bannerman writes in *The Church of Christ*, The Church is "the fulness of Him that filleth all in all."[2] Such an understanding compels the church planter to invest in the Church's growth, faithfully nurturing believers and encouraging them to become active, participating members of Christ's Body. The minister of the Gospel as church planter aims to see the Church flourish, not as a mere organization, but as the beloved bride of Christ, the "fullness" of Christ, radiant with His truth and love.

PRAYER

O God of all the nations of the earth,
   Remember the multitudes created in your image but unaware of your Son's redeeming work.
   Grant that, through the prayers and labors of your holy Church,
   They may be brought to know and worship you
   as revealed in Jesus Christ,
   Who lives and reigns with you and the Holy Spirit,
   One God, forever and ever. Amen.
   (Book of Common Prayer for Missions)

QUESTIONS
FOR REFLECTION AND DISCUSSION

FOR CHAPTER FOUR

1. Why is the affirmation of a divine call so crucial for church planters?
2. How can a church planter balance personal ministry with investing in future leaders?
3. What does it mean for a church planter to be a theologian, and how does this shape his ministry?
4. In what ways does Paul's exhortation to Timothy reflect the necessity of boldness in confronting false doctrine?
5. How can a church planter cultivate a love for people while maintaining a sense of divine calling and responsibility?
6. How does a church planter's encounter with the Gospel shape his ministry and impact others?

———

SCRIPTURES
FOR MEDITATION AND MEMORIZATION

- "I planted, Apollos watered, but God gave the increase." (1 Corinthians 3:6 NKJV)
- "What man of you, having a hundred sheep, if he loses one of them, does not leave the ninety-nine in the wilderness, and go after the one which is lost until he finds it?" (Luke 15:4 NKJV)
- "For this reason I left you in Crete, that you should set in order the things that are lacking, and appoint elders in every city as I commanded you." (Titus 1:5 NKJV)
- "We give thanks to the God and Father of our Lord Jesus Christ, praying always for you, since we heard of your faith in Christ Jesus and of your love for all the saints; because of the hope which is laid up for you in heaven, of which you heard before in the word of the truth of the gospel." (Colossians 1:3-5 NKJV)

ADDITIONAL RESOURCES: BAUCKHAM, RICHARD. BIBLE AND MISSION: CHRISTIAN WITNESS IN A POSTMODERN WORLD. GRAND RAPIDS: BAKER ACADEMIC, 2004.

Additional Resources:

1. Bauckham, Richard. *Bible and Mission: Christian Witness in a Postmodern World.* Grand Rapids: Baker Academic, 2004.
2. Dever, Mark. *The Church: The Gospel Made Visible.* Nashville: B&H Publishing Group, 2012.
3. Helm, David R. *Expositional Preaching: How We Speak God's Word Today.* Wheaton, IL: Crossway, 2014.
4. Allen, Roland. *Missionary Methods: St. Paul's or Ours?* Grand Rapids: Eerdmans, 1962.
5. Piper, John. *Brothers, We Are Not Professionals: A Plea to Pastors for Radical Ministry.* Nashville: B&H Publishing Group, 2002.

5
THE PORTRAIT OF THE CHURCH PLANTER
PART TWO

"He chose David his servant and took him from the sheepfolds; from following the nursing ewes he brought him to shepherd Jacob his people, Israel his inheritance. With upright heart he shepherded them and guided them with his skillful hand" (Psalm 78:70-72 ESV).

This chapter continues Paul's teachings to Timothy and expands on the traits essential for church planters, grounding them in Scripture and pastoral wisdom. The work of a church planter is sacred, involving both theological depth and practical ministry that reflects Christ's image.

16-39: FURTHER TRAITS OF A CHURCH PLANTER

16. A CHURCH PLANTER AS THE INCARNATIONAL REPOSITORY OF GODLINESS

Paul underscores the mystery of godliness in 1 Timothy 3:16, expressing the profound calling for church planters to embody and uphold the sacred truths of the Gospel: "And without controversy great is the mystery of godliness." This mystery is not something hidden but fully revealed in Christ Jesus. Godliness, therefore, is not external or superficial; it begins within, rooted in a heart transformed by obedience and gratitude to God's grace. The mystery of godliness is unveiled in the Old Testament and fully realized in the Lord Jesus. Thus, Dr. George Knight wrote:

> "Paul now writes of the confessed grandeur of the gospel in terms of him who is its reality. It is the revelation (μυστήριον) of true godliness (εὐσεβείας), a godliness seen and known in Jesus Christ."[1]

Paul demonstrates this with what appears to have been a fragment of a hymn or a creedal statement.[2] The "grandeur of the Gospel" is:

> He was manifested in the flesh,
>   vindicated by the Spirit,
>   seen by angels,
>   proclaimed among the nations,
>   believed on in the world,
>   taken up in glory.

Consider the mystery of godliness at work in the lives of God's people, which is the call of the passage and our concern for those who are Christian shepherds:

Deuteronomy 6:20-25: "When your son asks you in time to come, 'What is the meaning of the testimonies and the statutes and the rules that the Lord our God has commanded you?' then you shall say to your son, 'We were Pharaoh's slaves in Egypt. And the Lord brought us out of Egypt with a mighty hand... And the Lord commanded us to do all these statutes, to fear the Lord our God, for our good always, that he might preserve us alive, as we are this day.'"

- God's deliverance of Israel from bondage in Egypt—His gracious intervention to bring them from death to life—compels the people to respond with grateful obedience to His commands. Their obedience arises not from obligation alone but from remembering His mercy and goodness.

Romans 12:1: "I appeal to you therefore, brothers, by the mercies of God, to present your bodies as a living sacrifice, holy and acceptable to God, which is your spiritual worship."

- Here, mercy leads to obedience, and obedience becomes true worship—offering one's whole self (with attention to the body—σῶμα, *sōma*—and holiness by grace in one's use of the body) to God.[3] This obedience transcends mere rule-keeping; it is powered not by sheer will but by a spirit transformed through grace. As Jesus taught in the Sermon on the Mount, God's law penetrates deeply, revealing the call for both body and soul to be conformed to His will through grace (Matthew 5:21-22, 27-28).

The mystery of godliness, made manifest in Christ, calls the church planter to live as a visible reflection of the transformative power of the Gospel. This begins in his own life—a life of dependence upon the Lord, bearing fruit as an offering of gratitude for the grace he has received. As the Apostle Paul writes elsewhere, "It is no longer I who live, but Christ who lives in me" (Galatians 2:20). This Christ-centered life must radiate outward, influencing those he leads and serves.

The church planter, then, becomes a godly shepherd, serving the Master as a "good shepherd" (John 10:11–15) who guides others from the bondage of sin into the freedom of life in Christ (Romans 6:18), offering them a living example of holiness that is both accessible and authentic (Philippians 3:17). He leads by example, illustrating to his flock that godliness is indeed "profitable for all things, having promise of the life that now is and of that which is to come" (1 Timothy 4:8). Through his teaching and his life, he reveals that godliness is neither a set of rules nor moral performance, but the joyful, Spirit-filled expression of a life redeemed by Christ (Galatians 5:22–23; 2 Corinthians 3:17).

17. A Discerning Pastor

Paul warns Timothy of spiritual threats, cautioning him about false teachers who would lead others astray (1 Timothy 4:1-3). Church planters must possess this same discernment to recognize and protect their congregations from deception. Discernment is wisdom applied in vocational faithfulness, essential in all ministry but uniquely challenging in church planting, where a new, covenanted community forms around the life of our Lord Jesus Christ. Some may come to the church plant with unsuccessful schemes from other assemblies, seeing this emerging community as a testing ground for their novel ideas. Others may join, harboring an underlying aversion to authority, hoping to influence or destabilize the group.

A church plant, with its accessibility and openness, often attracts disaffected souls seeking a fresh start—some well-intentioned but wounded, others drawn by darker motives. The church planter, more accessible than a settled pastor of a larger congregation, is vulnerable to the challenges these individuals present. Thus, discernment must serve as both a shepherd's staff and a watchman's eye, safeguarding the congregation and upholding the integrity of the mission. As Paul cautions the Ephesian elders, "I know that after my departure fierce wolves will come in among you, not sparing the flock" (Acts 20:29). The church planter must be vigilant, grounded in wisdom, to discern and defend against threats, ensuring that the young community flourishes in Christ's love and truth.

18. Well-Trained in the Grandeur of the Gospel

Consider the veritable job description for Timothy in the passage:

"If you put these things before the brothers, you will be a good servant of Christ Jesus, being trained in the words of the faith and of the good doctrine that you have followed. Have nothing to do with irreverent, silly myths. Rather train yourself for godliness; for while bodily training is of some value, godliness is of value in every way, as it holds promise for the present life and also for the life to come." (1 Timothy 4:6–8, ESV)

From this Pauline admonition, we mark the mandate to Timothy and us:

- Keep the Gospel of God's grace in the resurrected and ascended Christ before the People. Gather in disciples of Jesus Christ by lifting Him as the fulfillment of the mystery of godliness.
- The life of our Lord is the starting point for continued training in God's grace and, thus, the Gospel's central message. Preach Him. Live by His power. Conform your life to His by the power of the Holy Spirit.

- Train yourself in spiritual disciplines to produce inner strength and growth in grace and truth.
- Focus on the heavenly things so you might be joyful in this life. This faith for dying and resurrecting is a "faith for living."

These directives root the church planter in the "grandeur of the Gospel," upholding truth, living by the power of Christ, and offering a "faith for living" that embraces both present and eternal promises. Bannerman reminds us that the church is "founded in grace, not in nature," existing as a divine society distinct from secular structures and thus being pastorally guarded against interference by worldly ambitions.[4] The church planter is a servant trained for godliness, faithful in teaching others to look beyond earthly concerns to the glory of Christ's Kingdom.

19. Focused on the Main Things

We should continue with the truths from 1 Timothy 4:6–8 related to the church planter's work. Paul's obvious concern in 1 Timothy 4:6–8 is that Timothy works smartly to avoid entanglement in likely distractions. What are they? Here, Paul points to *irreverent, silly myths.* This admonition should be of great concern to the pastor in missionary work. European Christianity, like other ethnic expressions to follow, sometimes syncretized pre-Christian myth with the Gospel. Of course, to add or subtract from the Gospel of the Lord Jesus Christ, as summarized, e.g., in the Apostles Creed, is to nullify the power of the Gospel. The Gospel is profound in its simplicity. Was Paul referring to irreverent, silly myths associated with the Judaizers? Paul urged Titus to be careful of such distractions, as well, and there denotes the kind of myths to avoid:

". . . not devoting themselves to Jewish myths and the commands of people who turn away from the truth. To the pure, all things are pure, but to the defiled and unbelieving, nothing is pure; but both their minds and their consciences are defiled" (Titus 1:14-15).

Mixing fanciful imaginations of so-called expert Jewish rabbis—allegory, numerology, astrology, and inserting mythological figures into Biblical truths—with the clear teaching of the Bible defiles the teacher, the text, and the community. Arguing about such things is to keep them alive and give them fuel for protracted arguments. To ignore those spreading false teachings and allow them to infest the tender seedlings of a new Christian assembly is to, likewise, enable adversaries to reroute the trajectory of the church. So what shall we do? Paul instructs Timothy to παραιτοῦ (paraitou) have nothing to do" with such tall tales. "Refuse" (1 Timothy 5:11) to engage with others in such talk.

> "Rather train yourself for godliness; for while bodily training is of some value, godliness is of value in every way, as it holds promise for the present life and also for the life to come" (1 Timothy 4:7–9 ESV).

To γύμναζε (train, exercise, as an Olympian would do) is to reroute the energy otherwise wasted on silly myths that introduce and stir trouble in the congregation into spiritual and pastoral practices that yield the fruit of peace through Biblical wisdom. Of course, this instruction is a first-level response. It is not the end-all in dealing with such evil. Paul writes elsewhere about confronting false teaching (see, e.g., 1 Timothy 1:3-4):

"that you may charge certain persons not to teach any different doctrine, nor to devote themselves to myths and endless genealogies, which promote speculations rather than the stewardship from God that is by faith" (ESV).

The force of Paul's words here is to teach pastors, church planters, and all Gospel ministers to address false teaching promptly, diffusing it before it can escalate into a situation requiring the exhausting work of formal discipline. Why spend more time here? Because Paul's warning about "silly myths" serves as an enduring guide for evangelists, reminding us of the mission-disrupting tactics that can creep into the church. Whether the meddling arises from the adversary (1 Peter 5:8), the flesh (Romans 8:5-8), or the world (1 John 2:16), the phenomenon of distorting the truth through a blend of biblical language and extraneous, misleading material is all too familiar.

This principle extends beyond false teaching alone; it applies to any attack that diverts the church planter from his primary work. The evangelist must hold a steady gaze on the Gospel of God, expressed through three main avenues: Word, Sacrament, and Prayer.

- **Word**: As Paul exhorts Timothy, "Preach the word; be ready in season and out of season; reprove, rebuke, and exhort, with complete patience and teaching" (2 Timothy 4:2 ESV). This encompasses preaching, Bible studies, counseling, writing, and proclaiming Christ through every means possible. Faithfully delivering the Word nurtures the souls in one's care and provides a firm anchor for a fledgling congregation.
- **Sacraments**: The two sacraments—baptism and the Lord's Supper—visibly manifest Christ's salvation and ongoing presence among His people. These are not mere rituals; they are means by which the grace of Christ is tangibly

affirmed in the church community. The church planter represents Christ in administering these sacraments, embodying a "ministry of presence" that reassures the people of God's nearness and promises.

- **Prayer**: Paul urges us to pray "at all times in the Spirit, with all prayer and supplication" (Ephesians 6:18 ESV), underscoring the vitality of a life steeped in prayer—public, private, group, and counseling prayers. For the church planter, prayer is the lifeblood of both ministry and personal holiness, creating a continual dependence upon God's guidance, wisdom, and strength.

These three foundational elements are essential for outreach and growth in grace and the sanctification of the church planter himself. In staying anchored to the Word, Sacraments, and Prayer, the church planter fosters a Gospel-centered community resilient against distractions and deviations from its mission. Through this intentional focus, he safeguards his ministry's purity and shepherds his people into deeper communion with Christ.

20. A Man of Holiness

As we have seen in 1 Timothy 4_6-7, Paul admonishes Timothy to respond to trouble in the church by pursuing personal holiness, which is central to the work of a church planter, as his ministry is an extension of his sanctification.

In the West (and particularly in English-speaking nations), in the twentieth and twenty-first centuries, we have witnessed the unwise introduction of new and popular, non-canonical motifs into the study and practice of church planting. These have included "the church planter as an entrepreneur," "the church planter as a corporate manager," "the church planter as a self-help guru," and "the church planter as the celebrity speaker." It should not need to be said that these are unBiblical and, therefore, wrong. Because they are bad, such assumed roles have disastrous consequences for all involved. As we know, "ideas have consequences." So, assuming borrowed roles alien to the mission of the evangelist or pastor will lead to distorted results at best. Naturally, the roles lend themselves to numerical, financial, and fame. Our Lord has made His pronouncement on these: "... Truly, I say to you, they have received their reward" (Matthew 6:2).

Yet, the role of the shepherd is incompatible with these assumed metaphors for the mission. The church planter must know the appropriate metaphor for his work and carefully study these in Scripture to avoid false identities. Without a caveat, we recommend the masterful study of the late John Stott: *The Preacher's Portrait*.[5] In it, the famed Anglican pastor and scholar identified the five Biblical identities that we must seek as patterns for our work:

1 *A Steward*: A keeper of the mysteries of the Gospel;

2 *A Herald*: A proclaimer of the Gospel;

3 *A Witness*: A living testimony to the reality and transformative power of the resurrected, ascended, and reigning Christ;

4 *A Father*: A Christian shepherd who relates to the flock of the Lord out of love, not, e.g., out of authoritarianism or with managerial detachment.

5 *A Servant*: The chief quality of a leader and the necessary posture of the Christian evangelist and shepherd.[6]

21. A Pilgrim with a Heavenly Vision

Like Bunyan's Pilgrim in the classic work, the church planter sees his work as part of a larger, eternal mission, striving toward the heavenly city.[7] The church planter enters a community and casts a vision for a future that is out of this world yet has now entered it. He has such faith in what God is doing with His kingdom that he preaches as if it is already here, and those who hear must come aboard the train to glory.

Soon, others gather around this strange man with his compelling vision of a God who is there, a God who is here, and a kingdom that has come. Some see it. Others gather to wait and see. Some come and depart. Yet through this necessary stage of examination and drawing of the elect of God, a covenanted Christian community forms amid the larger community. The eternal kingdom becomes visible within the gates of the earthly kingdom.

Guided by the Spirit of God in Christ, this is the church planter's exercise of "vision," and this is the inevitable outcome.

22. A Diligent Laborer

Throughout the Pastoral Epistles, Paul stresses the necessity of hard work. Laziness and self-pity are enemies of the church planter's work. Diligence in ministry is critical for the survival and growth of the church.

Read the "Excursus on Hard Work in the Pastoral Epistles" in Appendix 5.

23. An Authoritative Teacher of the Word

A church planter must command and teach God's Word with authority, as Paul instructs in 1 Timothy 4:11.

24. An Example to the Flock

Timothy is charged to be an example in speech, conduct, love, faith, and purity (1 Timothy 4:12). A church planter's life must reflect his teachings.

25. Gifted in Public Ministry

The public ministry of the Word is essential, and the church planter must devote himself to preaching, teaching, and exhorting (1 Timothy 4:13).

26. A Cultivator of His Gifts

Timothy is urged not to neglect his gifts but to immerse himself in ministry (1 Timothy 4:14-16). The church planter must constantly seek to grow and refine his God-given abilities.

27. Sanctification Through Vocation

The church planter's work is a means of sanctification, a reflection of his own spiritual journey.

28. Wise in Relationships with All Generations and Genders

Paul gives Timothy specific instructions on relating to older men, younger men, women, and others in the church (1 Timothy 5:1-2).

29. A Supporter of Family Life

The church planter must help build up family life within the church, honoring the roles of widows, parents, and children (1 Timothy 5:3-8).

30. A Man of Honor

Church planters labor honorably in preaching and teaching, as Paul highlights in 1 Timothy 5:17.

31. A Discerning Judge

A church planter must be wise and discerning in handling disputes and making judgments within the church (1 Timothy 5:21-25).

32. Careful in Selecting Ministry Partners

Paul warns Timothy not to be hasty in laying hands on others (1 Timothy 5:22). The church planter must carefully select those who share in ministry.

33. Attentive to His Own Health

In 1 Timothy 5:23, Paul encourages Timothy to care for his physical health. Church planters must care for their bodies as part of serving the Lord.

34. An Encourager of Christian Role Relationships

Church planters should encourage members to honor their role relationships, such as between slaves and masters (1 Timothy 6:1-2).

35. Content with Christ

The church planter must resist the temptation to pursue wealth or power, focusing instead on godliness and contentment (1 Timothy 6:3-10).

36. Pursuer of Godliness

Timothy is instructed to pursue righteousness, godliness, faith, love, steadfastness, and gentleness (1 Timothy 6:11). These virtues should characterize the church planter's life.

37. A Vision for Eternity

The church planter's vision is focused on eternity, keeping the commandment of Christ until His return (1 Timothy 6:12-16).

38. A Teacher of Generosity

The church planter should instruct the rich in the congregation to be generous and ready to share (1 Timothy 6:17-19).

39. A Trustee of the Gospel

Paul's final charge to Timothy is to guard the deposit of the Gospel (1 Timothy 6:20-21). The church planter must be a faithful steward of the truth.

PRAYER

O God and Father of all,
　　Whom the whole heavens adore,
　　Let the whole earth also worship You,
　　All nations obey You,
　　All tongues confess and bless You,
　　And men and women everywhere
　　Love and serve You in peace;
　　Through Jesus Christ our Lord. Amen.
　　(Book of Common Prayer for Missions)

QUESTIONS
FOR REFLECTION AND DISCUSSION

FOR CHAPTER FIVE

1. Why is discernment essential in the life of a church planter, especially regarding spiritual threats?
2. How does personal holiness impact a church planter's ministry?
3. What does it mean for a church planter to maintain a heavenly vision?
4. How can a church planter balance diligence in ministry with care for his spiritual and physical well-being?
5. In what ways can a church planter encourage generosity within his congregation?
6. Why is it important for church planters to cultivate their God-given gifts and avoid spiritual complacency?

SCRIPTURES
FOR MEDITATION AND MEMORIZATION

"And He Himself gave some to be apostles, some prophets, some evangelists, and some pastors and teachers, for the equipping of the saints for the work of ministry, for the edifying of the body of Christ, till we all come to the unity of the faith and of the knowledge of the Son of God, to a perfect man, to the measure of the stature of the fullness of Christ; that we should no longer be children, tossed to and fro and carried about with every wind of doctrine, by the trickery of men, in the cunning craftiness of deceitful plotting." (Ephesians 4:11-14 NKJV)

ADDITIONAL RESOURCES

1. Gentry, Peter J., and Stephen J. Wellum. *Kingdom through Covenant: A Biblical-Theological Understanding of the Covenants.* Wheaton, IL: Crossway, 2012.
2. Dever, Mark. *Nine Marks of a Healthy Church.* Wheaton, IL: Crossway, 2013.
3. Helm, David. *1 & 2 Timothy and Titus: To Guard the Deposit.* Wheaton, IL: Crossway, 2015.
4. Horton, Michael. *The Gospel Commission: Recovering God's Strategy for Making Disciples.* Grand Rapids: Baker Books, 2011.
5. Marshall, Colin, and Tony Payne. *The Trellis and the Vine: The Ministry Mind-Shift That Changes Everything.* Kingsford, Australia: Matthias Media, 2009.
6. Payne, J. D. *Apostolic Church Planting.* Downers Grove, IL: IVP Press, 2015.

6

THE PORTRAIT OF THE CHURCH PLANTER
PART THREE

"He will feed His flock like a shepherd; He will gather the lambs with His arm, and carry them in His bosom, and gently lead those who are with young" (Isaiah 40:11 NKJV).

In Paul's final epistle, written while he awaited execution in Rome, he calls Timothy to come to him. In it, he highlights key truths for church planters, especially regarding the challenges of ministry.

CONTINUING TRAITS OF A CHURCH PLANTER

40. Subject to Isolation

Church planting can be lonely, as Paul's imprisonment shows. Yet, in the long shadows of disquieting solitude, reaching a man's interior, the planter must seek the Lord sincerely, becoming what he will preach in public. How so? You need not fight against isolation. You need not pretend to prefer it to the company of others. You can release your anxiety about isolation by drawing near to God in prayer. I do not mean to heartlessly suggest that you have a stiff upper lip and get on with it, but that in some sense and by an incomprehensible providence, isolation becomes a strange gift. To receive the gift of suffering is to remove the poison from the provocation. God is cultivating your inner life so that you may all the more be authentically you, the man God has called to proclaim the unsearchable riches of Christ in public.

41. Used by God Despite Appearances

Even when the work appears to falter, when every outward sign points to failure, God's hand is often at its most mysterious. Like Paul, whose ministry seemed repeatedly threatened by adversity, the church planter is shaped not in moments of ease but in the crucible of hardship. It is in these very trials—when success feels distant—that God refines both the planter and the church, molding them for purposes unseen, using what looks like defeat to bring forth a greater victory.

42. Lives and Dies by God's Promises

Like Paul, the church planter must cling to the promises of God, living in the reality of eternal life already at work within him (2 Timothy 1:1). Paul's words, "the promise of life which is in Christ Jesus," are both grounding and instructive. For the man of God called to establish a Gospel community, this promise of life must be the centerpiece of his preaching and ministry. It calls the planter to recognize the paradox of eternity breaking into the fragile, fleeting world of the temporal. And yet, it is precisely this promise of eternal life—central to both the message and the planter's own existence—that guards him from the lure of building an earthly kingdom. Even if he tried, he could not. The need for eternal life is both unsettling and comforting. For to proclaim the promise of life in Christ is to announce it before the very gates of darkness and even before the reality of judgment. The church planter's message—the need for eternal life through faith in the crucified, resurrected, ascended, and returning Christ Jesus, the promised Messiah to Israel and to all the world—marks him as a man bearing a word from another world. His proclamation transcends the temporal, pointing beyond the immediate and the visible.

In the same way, the community he gathers is more than just a congregation—it is a glimpse of eternity, a living sign from God to those still rooted in the passing realities of this world. It stands as a quiet yet profound witness, calling the lost to something far greater than the here and now. To be this man, to preach this message, and to gather these souls by enfolding them into the life of following Jesus is to enjoy the fullness of Paul's words: "Grace, mercy, *and* peace from God the Father and Christ Jesus our Lord."

43. Devout in Prayer

Paul's life is a living testament to the power of constant prayer (2 Timothy 1:3). A deep-rooted church plant depends on a planter tethered to Christ through fervent, regular communion with God. When the Apostle says, "I thank God, whom I serve with a pure conscience, as my forefathers did, as without ceasing I remember you in my prayers night and day," he is not only giving thanks but also alerting Timothy to the vital necessity of prayer. For the church planter, this necessity arises from the unseen yet powerful forces at work as the Gospel is proclaimed.

We would not cease pleading with God in prayer if we could only glimpse the spiritual battle beyond the thin veil separating this present age from eternity. We would urge others to join us in intercession, knowing that prayer is a weapon and a lifeline. Does this not testify to its power? In His mercy, God delights to hear and respond to prayer. We acknowledge our utter dependence on the living Savior in devout and humble prayer. And more, through prayer, we are shaped and transformed by the dynamic exchange between heaven and earth.

If you respond to this reality by merely designing and distributing prayer supporter cards, you will receive the hollow fruit of such superficiality. Prayer is not a perfunctory task on a business plan checklist. The cry for prayer is the cry of a man who understands that he is carrying forth the very kingdom of God—a kingdom that will most certainly provoke fierce resistance from the forces of evil. And that cry will ring out to the would-be community of Christ in that place: "We are about God's work here. And we must do God's work in God's way. I need prayer—or I am at the mercy of spiritual forces far beyond my strength. Pray to the living God for our deliverance, that we may freely proclaim the name of Jesus in this place."

44. Loves People Passionately

Paul's longing to see Timothy (2 Timothy 1:4) reveals the very heart of a church planter. There is a pulsating pathos within this simple sentence: "greatly desiring to see you, being mindful of your tears, that I may be filled with joy." The work of church planting is profoundly relational, driven by love—a love that binds souls together in the labor of the Gospel. Paul does not overlook Timothy's tears. He acknowledges them, knowing they speak of trials, of the crushing weight of ministry that often feels like defeat—a wounded shepherd lying amidst the stench of despair. And yet, Timothy's tears do not dissuade Paul. Far from seeing them as a failure, Paul recognizes them as part of the journey, for he himself has known such moments, facing despair "even unto death" (2 Corinthians 1:8).

In these opening words, Paul is already at work—teaching, guiding, and pouring the healing balm of the Gospel into the wounds of a fellow shepherd. Like all pastoral work in this "present evil age" (Galatians 1:4), church planting is not for the faint of heart. It demands a resilience born of grace. But Paul's longing for Timothy, for the joy that would come from seeing him spiritually restored, reflects more than human affection. It is a glimpse of the love of Christ, the Good Shepherd, who intercedes for His own. How much more does our Redeemer long for your joy and pray for your strength as you labor in His field?

45. Empowered by the Faith of Others

Timothy's faith did not spring from nowhere; it was a seed planted long before, nurtured in the quiet fidelity of his grandmother and mother (2 Timothy 1:5-7). Their witness shaped him, not in loud declarations, but in the steady rhythm of lives lived before God. And so it is with the church planter—his work is never truly his own. He draws on the faith handed down to him, the unseen hands of those who prayed and believed before him. He must pass that fragile yet eternal flame to others, fanning it into something greater than himself.

46. Shares in Suffering for the Gospel

Church planting carries an inevitable share of suffering for the Gospel, as Paul warned Timothy (2 Timothy 1:8). It's not a mark of failure but a necessary companion to the work woven into the very fabric of ministry. Easy to state but hard to learn, this truth unfolds slowly—etched deeply into the heart through the trials that test a planter's resolve and faith, reminding him that such suffering is part of the cost of proclaiming Christ.

47. Ministry Fueled by a Holy Calling

Paul reminds us that the work of a church planter is born not of human effort but from a holy calling, a gift of grace (2 Timothy 1:9). Vocation is not merely the beginning of Gospel ministry; it is the unquenchable fire in the very center of our personhood—the burning bush—that shapes the planter's life. Vocation is the inescapable voice of God—woven through providence and conscience—that draws you forward. This calling is the spark that ignites the journey and the steady flame that fuels the long, often arduous road of faithful service.

48. Grounded in the Gospel of Christ

A church planter's ministry must be anchored in the life, death, and resurrection of Jesus (2 Timothy 1:10). How could it be otherwise? Jesus is our all in all. If church planting veers into another lane along the way, the enterprise will most certainly turn to the wrong destination. The God-man, Christ Jesus, is the Alpha and Omega of church planting. He must be exalted as the way, the truth, and the life. He must be lifted up through the divinely prescribed means of grace He has given us.

49. Guards the Gospel with Faith and Love

The church planter is called to guard the Gospel, ensuring it remains pure and untainted by false teachings (2 Timothy 1:13-14). This is no passive task. The Good Shepherd is not weak but a strong laborer fiercely devoted to the well-being of the flock. And so, the church planter—by which we mean the Christian pastor undertaking the sacred mission of establishing new communities of disciples through Word, Sacrament, and Prayer—must vigilantly examine all expressions of ministry arising from the gathered community. In time, a plurality of elders will share in the oversight of this Gospel work, but in its infancy, the planter is tasked with a John Knox-like superintendency over the new flock. Yet, his role is not that of a warden overseeing a penal colony. Instead, it is the way of the Good Shepherd—one who guards this sacred work with faith in Christ and love for both God and His elect.

50. Grounded in Sound Words of Scripture

The church must be built on the unchanging foundation of

Scripture, and it falls to the church planter to ensure that its teachings remain faithful to God's Word (2 Timothy 1:13-14). As Paul instructs Timothy: "Hold fast the pattern of sound words which you have heard from me, in faith and love which are in Christ Jesus. That good thing which was committed to you, keep by the Holy Spirit who dwells in us." The weight of this charge rests squarely on the shoulders of the church planter. The burden of fidelity—to shepherd the flock according to Christ's ways—is his to bear.

Yet, this faithfulness is not achieved by human effort alone. Paul reminds us that it is through the Holy Spirit that we are able to keep the truth. What does this mean for the church planter? It means that we must seek God with all our being, prioritizing the kingdom of Christ above all else. The Holy Spirit, who always honors the Son, strengthens us when Christ is exalted in our lives. In this way, our efforts to remain faithful are not only supported but made sure by the Spirit of God. The planter's steadfastness is anchored in the divine power that works within him, ensuring the truth remains unshaken.

51. Refreshed by Fellowship

This passage from the Pastoral Epistles offers a revealing glimpse into the work of ministry that St. Paul undertook:

> "This you know, that all those in Asia have turned away from me, among whom are Phygellus and Hermogenes. The Lord grant mercy to the household of Onesiphorus, for he often refreshed me, and was not ashamed of my chain; but when he arrived in Rome, he sought me out very zealously and found me. The Lord grant to him that he may find mercy from the Lord in that Day—and you know very well how many ways he ministered to me at Ephesus" (2 Timothy 1:15-18).

Not only do we gain insight into Paul's grim situation in

Rome—where Onesiphorus sought and encouraged him during his imprisonment—but Paul also reflects on the history of the church plant at Ephesus. He reminds Timothy of how helpful Onesiphorus had been there, showing that this man's ministry of refreshment was not a one-time act but part of his ongoing service to the body of Christ.

Church planting often carries the painful wound of isolation. Loneliness can settle heavily on the soul of the planter. Yet here, we see how God, in His providence, led a faithful saint into Paul's life to refresh him. This is a reminder: be on the lookout for those "angels unaware"—friends or supporters you may not even know today—whom the Holy Spirit will send to your aid.

And remember that our ultimate pattern is the Lord Jesus Christ. After His forty days and nights in the scorching desert, He, too, was ministered to by angels (Matthew 4:11). We have spoken of the reality of demonic activity in spiritual warfare; let us also not forget the equally real presence of angelic assistance. God knows your needs and will direct both men and heavenly creatures to your side. So, be not afraid, and be not dismayed. The Lord is with you.

52. Strengthened by God's Grace

Church planters must live out of God's grace, yielding to Him so Church planters must live from the wellspring of God's grace, yielding to His strength as the source that sustains them: "You therefore, my son, be strong in the grace that is in Christ Jesus" (2 Timothy 2:1). Recall how David, in the midst of despair, "encouraged himself in the Lord" (1 Samuel 30:6), and how Peter exhorts us to "humble yourselves under the mighty hand of God, that He may exalt you in due time" (1 Peter 5:6). The Scriptures are filled with examples of those who, because of their service to God, faced profound adversity. And what was their anchor in these storms? It was the unshakable grace of God.

This grace is not merely the message you proclaim to others—it is the divine fuel that ignites your own life and ministry. God has sent His only begotten Son to live the life you could not live and to die the death you deserved. That truth is not just for the pulpit; it is the heartbeat of your soul. This Gospel of grace is the divine fission at the core of your being, bringing power to both life and service. Grace is the stabilizing agent, the homeostasis of the soul, giving life and energy even when weakness threatens to overwhelm. For the source of this strength is not of this world but from the eternal God who calls and sustains you.

53. Ministry Multiplier

Church planters are not only called to establish new communities but also to raise up faithful men who will carry on the work of Gospel ministry: "And the things that you have heard from me among many witnesses, commit these to faithful men who will be able to teach others also" (2 Timothy 2:2). In every expression of pastoral ministry, the minister must be praying for and watching for those whom God is calling as future servants. Church planting, perhaps the most demanding field in the spectrum of Christian shepherding, requires this all the more.

The work is too great for one person alone, and God, in His wisdom, gifts the church with men who will continue the mission. As church planters, we must actively seek out those gifted by God to go and preach the Gospel in places where the church does not yet exist or in growing communities where the need for a Gospel presence is evident. The future of the church rests in part on this faithful multiplication as the next generation of ministers rises to gather new Gospel communities and shepherd them in Christ's name.

PRAYER

O God, the strength of all who put their trust in You,
    Mercifully accept our prayers;
    And because in our weakness, we can do nothing good without You,
    Give us the help of Your grace,
    that in keeping Your commandments
    We may please You both in will and deed;
    through Jesus Christ our Lord,
    Who lives and reigns with You and the Holy Spirit,
    One God, forever and ever. Amen.
    (Book of Common Prayer, For Strength)

QUESTIONS
FOR REFLECTION AND DISCUSSION

FOR CHAPTER SIX

1. How does Paul's isolation in prison inform our understanding of the loneliness of church planting?
2. In what ways does adversity refine both the planter and the church? How have you seen this in ministry?
3. Why is it essential for church planters to live by the promises of God's Word?
4. How can a church planter's prayer life sustain the work of planting deep-rooted churches?
5. What role does the faith of others play in encouraging church planters, both personally and in their mentoring of others?
6. How can church planters balance suffering for the Gospel with remaining faithful and hopeful in their calling?

SCRIPTURES
FOR MEDITATION AND MEMORIZATION

- ChatGPT
- "So then neither he who plants is anything, nor he who waters, but God who gives the increase" (1 Corinthians 3:7 NKJV).
- "From Miletus he sent to Ephesus and called for the elders of the church" (Acts 20:17 NKJV).
- "And a vision appeared to Paul in the night. A man of Macedonia stood and pleaded with him, saying, 'Come over to Macedonia and help us'" (Acts 16:9 NKJV).
- "Strengthening the souls of the disciples, exhorting them to continue in the faith, and saying, 'We must through many tribulations enter the kingdom of God'" (Acts 14:22 NKJV).

———

ADDITIONAL RESOURCES

1. Allen, Roland. *The Ministry of the Spirit.* Grand Rapids: Eerdmans, 1960.
2. Carson, D.A. *A Call to Spiritual Reformation: Priorities from Paul and His Prayers.* Grand Rapids: Baker Academic, 1992.
3. Bridges, Jerry. *The Discipline of Grace: God's Role and Our Role in the Pursuit of Holiness.* Colorado Springs: NavPress, 2006.
4. Piper, John. *The Supremacy of God in Preaching.* Grand Rapids: Baker Books, 2004.
5. Whitney, Donald S. *Spiritual Disciplines for the Christian Life.* Colorado Springs: NavPress, 1991.
6. Stott, John. *The Message of 2 Timothy: Guard the Gospel.* Downers Grove, IL: IVP Academic, 1973.

7
THE PORTRAIT OF THE CHURCH PLANTER
PART FOUR

"The Lord is my shepherd; I shall not want. He makes me to lie down in green pastures; He leads me beside the still waters. He restores my soul; He leads me in the paths of righteousness for His name's sake. Yea, though I walk through the valley of the shadow of death, I will fear no evil; for You are with me; Your rod and Your staff, they comfort me" (Psalm 23:1-4 NKJV).

In Paul's final epistle, as he faces martyrdom, we gain additional traits that characterize the life and ministry of a church planter based on his instructions to Timothy.

CONTINUING TRAITS OF A CHURCH PLANTER

54. Single-minded in Gospel Mission

Paul encourages Timothy to avoid becoming entangled in civilian pursuits: "No one engaged in warfare entangles himself with the affairs of this life, that he may please him who enlisted him as a soldier" (2 Timothy 2:4). In verses 4-7, we learn that a church planter's focus must be singular: advancing the Gospel and pleasing the One who called him into this work. Paul's words remind us that the planter, like a soldier, must stay undistracted by pursuits that do not serve the mission.

This, however, is not a dismissal of bi-vocational ministry. Paul himself supported his ministry through the work of his own hands, as he reminds the Thessalonians:

> "For you yourselves know how you ought to follow our example. We were not idle when we were with you, nor did we eat anyone's food without paying for it. On the contrary, we worked night and day, laboring and toiling so that we would not be a burden to any of you" (2 Thessalonians 3:7-8).

In Acts 18:3, we see Paul working as a tentmaker: "And because he was a tentmaker as they were, he stayed and worked with them."

Paul urges discernment here, calling Timothy to weigh every endeavor with a simple but piercing question: "Does this advance the Gospel for this mission?" Whether fully supported by the church or working another job to sustain the mission, the church planter's life must revolve around this singular aim: the proclamation of Christ and the building of His kingdom according to the Scriptures. As Paul also wrote, "Whatever you do, work at it with all your heart, as working for the Lord, not for human masters" (Colossians 3:23). Every effort, every action, must ultimately serve the advancement of the Gospel.

55. Sacrificial in Service for the Elect

Like Paul in 2 Timothy 2:8-10, the church planter endures hardship, even chains, for the sake of God's elect. His mission is to declare the resurrection of Jesus Christ so that those who are appointed to believe may hear the Gospel and obtain salvation in Christ Jesus: "Therefore I endure all things for the sake of the elect, that they also may obtain the salvation which is in Christ Jesus with eternal glory" (2 Timothy 2:10).

What an astounding truth: the man of God labors not only for the glory of God but for the sake of God's elect, those known and loved by the Father before the foundation of the world (Ephesians 1:4). The church planter is, in a sense, both bound and free. He is a slave to the mission, wrapped in velvet chains—chains that signify his complete surrender to Christ's call. He is an abused prophet, bruised by the world yet held in the tender arms of angels (Hebrews 1:14), all for the good of those he seeks to reach. His endurance is not in vain, for it is the means by which God's chosen ones hear the message that leads to life eternal.

56. Avoids Quarrels and Irreverent Babble

Paul warns Timothy against meaningless controversies that distract from the Gospel, urging him to remain focused on truth and the life it produces:

> "Remind them of these things, charging them before the Lord not to strive about words to no profit, to the ruin of the hearers. Be diligent to present yourself approved to God, a worker who does not need to be ashamed, rightly dividing the word of truth. But shun profane and idle babblings, for they will increase to more ungodliness. And their message will spread like cancer. Hymenaeus and Philetus are of this sort, who have strayed concerning the truth, saying that the resurrection is already past; and they overthrow the faith of some. Nevertheless the solid foundation of God stands, having this seal: 'The Lord knows those who are His,' and, 'Let everyone

who names the name of Christ depart from iniquity'" (2 Timothy 2:14-19).

Every Christian shepherd with any measure of experience recognizes the type of people Paul is speaking about. These are not seekers of peace or truth; they are agitators, rebels who thrive on chaos, or perhaps unqualified teachers who flood the community with unfounded claims and hollow theories that derail the pursuit of truth. And what of their message? Paul calls it cancerous, spreading unchecked through the body of believers. The unholy words from unbridled tongues infect the community, metastasizing into a foul growth that strangles the very life of a Gospel-centered church.

It would be wrong to dismiss every troublesome person with a simple, "There's the door." We are called to shepherd the wounded, even those who lash out from their pain. But what Paul describes here is something different. There are sheep. And there are goats—and most dangerously—wolves! We don't shepherd wolves. God may transform them (e.g., Saul of Tarsus) through our message from heaven, but wolves are a clear and present danger. Let the Christian shepherd be on guard and be so grounded in God's Word, guided by God's Spirit, that he recognizes the difference (their works will reveal their identity; see no. 58). When malicious men infiltrate the flock, delighting in disorder, spreading lies, and sowing division, the church planter must not hesitate in guarding the community. Paul's exhortation is clear: we must protect the flock from those who thrive on tearing down rather than building up. The life of a Gospel community is too precious to let it be overrun by those whose words are poison, darkening devotion, and spreading clouds of deception.

57. Engages in Restorative Discipline

The church planter does not dismiss all who fall into sin

but seeks to restore them through loving discipline, guiding them toward cleansing and honorable use in God's work. Some will respond immediately, while others may resist or walk away, only to be restored in another Christian community at another time. Yet, there are those whose transformation will occur before all, becoming living testimonies to the power of God's grace—grace that reaches even the most unlikely and despicable of souls.

> "But in a great house there are not only vessels of gold and silver, but also of wood and clay, some for honor and some for dishonor. Therefore if anyone cleanses himself from the latter, he will be a vessel for honor, sanctified and useful for the Master, prepared for every good work" (2 Timothy 2:20-21).

Even as Paul thunders against the wicked who infiltrate the church, he reminds Timothy that these are human souls—souls who, like Paul himself, may curse Christ one day and preach Him the next. This is the weight of pastoral ministry: the call to discernment and discipline, yet always with an eye toward restoration. What a demanding task this is, requiring both firmness and grace. And how can such supernatural work be accomplished by any means other than those provided by God Himself? Only through the Spirit's power can the church planter faithfully carry out the work of transforming broken vessels into ones of honor, sanctified and ready for the Master's use.

58. Discerns Between the Flock and Wolves

The topic of false teaching leads Paul to even greater depths of urgent warning:

"But know this, that in the last days perilous times will come: For men will be lovers of themselves, lovers of money, boasters, proud, blasphemers, disobedient to parents, unthankful, unholy, unloving, unforgiving, slanderers, without self-control, brutal, despisers of good, traitors, headstrong, haughty, lovers of pleasure rather than lovers of God, having a form of godliness but denying its power. And from such people turn away! For of this sort are those who creep into households and make captives of gullible women loaded down with sins, led away by various lusts, always learning and never able to come to the knowledge of the truth. Now as Jannes and Jambres resisted Moses, so do these also resist the truth: men of corrupt minds, disapproved concerning the faith; but they will progress no further, for their folly will be manifest to all, as theirs also was" (2 Timothy 3:1-9).

We need not speculate about 'the last days." For Paul, the resurrection and ascension of our Lord Jesus inaugurated a new era, "the last days." Christ, who is now crowned as Lord of Lords and King of Kings "at the right hand of God," is coming again. And therefore, we live in those last days. Every sign of these days was present when Paul wrote to Timothy. And yet, even as William Hendrisksen (1900-1982) reminds us in his masterful work on Revelation, *More than Conquerors,* the signs grow more pronounced as the years and the millennia roll on.[1] Or, as the Scripture reveals elsewhere, "as sin abounds, grace abounds more." So, each generation of Christian shepherds is bound to witness and have to address these spiritual maladies. Paul, here, speaks of those who have gone astray, like "Jannes and Jambres," who resisted Moses and Aaron in the royal courts of Pharaoh. Of these men, *Logos* summarizes:

In the context of resisting the truth, an article draws a parallel between Jannes and Jambres, who opposed Moses, and certain false teachers of Paul's time[1]. These names, though not found in the Old Testament, are understood to refer to the Egyptian magicians mentioned in Exodus 7-8[2]. The article notes that these individuals resist the truth, are described as "men of corrupt minds," and are "disapproved concerning the faith." Another source elaborates that Jannes and Jambres, like the false teachers, "played on superstitious susceptibilities with a plausibly presented parody of the truth"[2]. It's mentioned that their names appear in various forms in extra-biblical sources, including Jewish legends and pagan writings[2]. The text also states that these false teachers will not progress further, as their foolishness will become evident to all, just as it did with Jannes and Jambres[3][4].²

This powerful and essential passage shows us how to respond to opposition. Moses did not need to directly conflict with the court magicians who opposed God's Word and His servant. He acted in obedience to God's call—to proclaim the Gospel from that stage of redemptive history. In the same way, we overcome evil with good. Do what God has called you to do, and in time, the spiritual work will overwhelm the spirits, influencing those who resist.

This is not a shallow call to "preach louder," but rather a call for calm, deliberate, steady, and faithful administration of Word, Sacrament, and Prayer—both publicly and from house to house, as Paul demonstrated in Acts 20:20. Through this steady obedience, God's work is accomplished, even in the face of opposition.

59. Grounded in Scripture as the Inerrant Word of God

The church planter's ministry is built on the inerrancy and

sufficiency of Scripture. Only through the Word of God can a church planter teach and equip others for every good work (2 Timothy 3:16-17). Here is the defining factor in evaluating church planting ministries. It is the necessary line of demarcation between a human work and a divine movement of God in a place, in a time. The former does not prioritize Scripture as the arbitrator of the vision and mission, much less the strategic steps. It is a work of the hands without the anointing of God, which must accompany His Word to us, the Bible. The latter is a ministry grounded in glory, marked by hard work of the laborer's hands, but done according to Scripture, as if God were talking to the shepherd audibly. Thus, the power and mystery of Psalm 90:17 is at work in the church plant that is uncompromisingly Biblical:

> "And let the beauty of the Lord our God be upon us,
> And establish the work of our hands for us;
> Yes, establish the work of our hands."

I am sorry to say that in my ministry on behalf of Christ, I have deposited too much of myself and the world's ways into the communities we founded. I never waivered in my conviction and desire to labor according to the Word of God, yet when I look at the fruit of the work these years afterward, I can see something of me in certain places. And that I confess as a sinful, unholy addition to the spiritual fabric of the church. So even in the most dedicated founding work (not that mine was) we are likely to discover some idea, some preference, some eccentricity, that is unbiblical and, therefore, unnecessary and potentially harmful. So what can we do? We are but men. We pray. We ask God to show us ourselves. Self-awareness is a humanly difficult feature to secure. There is a veritable litany of reasons why we must pray earnestly and fervently, in public and private, for the work of the founding, but this one reason stands out in our study. This is why Paul will question the matter:

1 Corinthians 2:1
"And I, brethren, when I came to you, did not come with excellence of speech or of wisdom declaring to you the testimony of God."

Romans 16:25
"Now to Him who is able to strengthen you by my gospel and by the proclamation of Jesus Christ, according to the revelation of the mystery concealed for ages past."

1 Corinthians 1:17
"For Christ did not send me to baptize, but to preach the gospel, not with words of wisdom, lest the cross of Christ be emptied of its power."

1 Corinthians 2:4
"My message and my preaching were not with persuasive words of wisdom but with a demonstration of the Spirit's power,"

1 Corinthians 2:7
"No, we speak of the mysterious and hidden wisdom of God, which He destined for our glory before time began."

1 Corinthians 2:13
"And this is what we speak, not in words taught us by human wisdom, but in words taught by the Spirit, expressing spiritual truths in spiritual words."

60. Preaches in Season and Out of Season

Paul charges Timothy to preach the Word, regardless of popular opinion, with patience and sound teaching. A church planter must endure hardships while staying true to the Gospel (2 Timothy 4:1-5). "In season and out of season" means "all seasons!" You must preach from the day of the initial phase to the day you are removed by a divine call (to evangelize or to die). And no one will have to urge the church planter to preach. He is, first and foremost, a preacher of the Gospel. He preaches from the centering place of what God has done in Christ in his life. But the call if not just to indulge a predisposition to a gift or pattern of behaviors. This is a call to preach the truth of Scripture in every circumstance. If you believe this is easy or without pain, you have not preached "out of season." Remember that a church planter goes to a place because a community lives in a perpetual "out-of-season" existence. This is the burden that leads to the vision. And this burden for the out-of-season people is the fuel for the fission inside of the bosom of the church planter—a burning in the bones that cannot find release but by proclamation of the unsearchable riches of Christ.

To preach in this way, one must conduct serious and solemn planning (long-term) and preparation (short-term, i.e., the immediate time of preaching, e.g., the Monday through Saturday before the Lord's Day).

61. Ministers in Anticipation of Another World

This passage, 2 Timothy 4:6-8, is a critical one for church planters. This involves reading the context of ministry correctly. Read the passage very carefully:

> "For I am already being poured out like a drink offering, and the time of my departure is at hand. I have fought the good fight, I have finished the race, I have kept the faith. From now on, there is laid up for me the crown of righteousness, which the Lord, the righteous Judge, will award to me on that day—and not only to me, but to all who crave His appearing."

What do we learn? The church planter can misread his

context. He might think that a prison in Rome is a defeat or that a coming execution is an utterly failed way to conclude one's Gospel service. Next time you think you are not treated well, reflect on 2 Timothy 4:6-8. Remember that the context includes two dimensions of the same reality. You labor here. You labor in light of eternity.

Firstly, circumstances do not—can not—define success in Gospel ministry. Why? Because the context is incomplete. Our evaluation for ministry, firstly, comes from God, not ourselves or others. Secondly, we minister in light of eternity. We will appear before the Lord. Our crown of righteousness, our reward, is not here. That means you seek to establish this covenanted community of Christ Jesus with your eye on Him. As you do, those who will believe unto salvation will also follow your gaze. And would you want them to look elsewhere? Make your ministry one that is out of this world. Our reward is with God. Therefore, minister—preach, evangelize, disciple, make decisions—out of a reward before you, not a sword on your neck or, worse, a dollar at your feet (2 Timothy 4:6-8).

62. Endures Betrayal and Disloyalty

Paul experienced desertion from fellow laborers like Demas, yet he pressed on in his work for Christ. A church planter, likewise, will face betrayal, but this must not derail his mission. In 2 Timothy 4:9-10, Paul writes:

> "Do your best to come to me quickly, for Demas, because he loved this world, has deserted me and has gone to Thessalonica. Crescens has gone to Galatia, and Titus to Dalmatia."

Paul was not immune to such sorrows. He is a father in the faith, a pillar of the Church, but still fully human. We often forget that even those who stand as giants of faith are subject to the same temptations to despair as any of us. There is no sin or shame in the heartache of betrayal. Jesus Himself was betrayed by Judas and abandoned by all but John, who stood with Mary at the foot of the cross. Should we expect better? We might hope and pray for different outcomes, but the pattern of ministry, as evidenced throughout Scripture, often includes the deep and visceral pain of desertion.

Some reading this may feel that painful loneliness even now. It is a reality in all pastoral ministries but is especially acute in evangelistic outreach and church planting. Demas may have abandoned you for the allure of the world, but God has not. He is with you, which is why He promises, *"I will never leave you nor forsake you"* (Hebrews 13:5)—because such abandonment in this present age is common. The presence of God is your assurance and strength amidst every trial you shall face. Every church planter will inevitably undergo the refining school of trials.

63. Experiences Restoration of Broken Relationships

Despite the earlier division, Paul calls for John Mark to join him again in ministry. Church planters will witness how God can restore relationships for the sake of the Gospel's advancement. In 2 Timothy 4:11-12, Paul writes:

> "Only Luke is with me. Get Mark and bring him with you because he is useful to me in the ministry. Tychicus, however, I have sent to Ephesus."

There is something profoundly beautiful in these words. Paul's final remarks to Timothy reveal a tender reconciliation between him and John Mark, closing the chapter of their earlier conflict. This is a reminder that those who may walk away today could one day stand beside you in the darkest hours of your life. Always keep your heart open to the possibility of reunion, for God's power to bring about divine reconciliation is a testimony in itself. Repaired relationships are not just personal victories—they serve as living witnesses to God's grace and the unity of His Church.

Note also how Paul's mention of Mark seems to revive his spirit: *"Tychicus, however, I have sent to Ephesus"* (2 Timothy 4:12). The sorrow over desertion gives way to a renewed sense of mission through the faithfulness and unity found in restored relationships. Losses and disappointments naturally lead to reflection, but they remind us of God's ongoing work and the enduring bonds of fellowship. Faithfulness inspires an impulse to refocus on the mission at hand. So when caught in the briars of disunity, remember the faithfulness of those who remain and press forward in your calling. This mindset will restore joy and purpose amid any affliction or trial.

64. Is a Man in Need.

We must not suppose that the Apostle Paul is a superman, unaffected by the needs common to all men. Nor should we forget that we are creatures who feel love and, thus, the loss of love. We enjoy the company of others, especially those in the Body of Christ. All the more, then, do we experience the chilling isolation of a solitude unjustly imposed.

The Bible says it is not good for a man to be alone. Paul is either cold or anticipating the cold. Coldness heightens isolation. He is, in the end, a man who is alone with himself. But then he is all the more present with God. Yet he was but a man. The Apostle Paul was either never married or divorced (because of his conversion?) or possibly widowed. All we can say for sure is that there is no record of a family (other than his Benjamite line in Philippians 3:5).[3] And he is most certainly unmarried ("I wish that all were as I myself am" in 1 Corinthians 7:7) in this season of his life. Yet, the all-consuming ministry has now brought him to the cold and heartless cell of loneliness. "Keep warm. Read. Pray. Witness.

What are the remaining things that I can do for the mission before I depart?" Such were the likely musings of the great *Apostle of the Heart Set Free.*[4]

So, Saint Paul directs Pastor Timothy to go through the northwestern part of Asia Minor to Troas to retrieve his cloak, presumably from a Christian there.[5,6] Paul's request for his books and parchments (or the book, i.e., the Old Testament Bible, above all the ones that are parchment, see Knight in footnote 3) shows that a church planter must be a constant student of Scripture, nurturing his ministry with sound knowledge (2 Timothy 4:13): "When you come, bring the cloak that I left with Carpus at Troas, also the books, and above all the parchments."

Like the Apostle Paul, we are men utterly dependent on God's comfort to sustain us—in body and soul, in emotion, and in contemplation. We preach Christ, yet we are also called to bear, in some measure, the weight of His awe-inspiring and sorrowful cross. The very things Paul requests are those we, too, instinctively long for in our inevitable seasons of isolation—an abandonment endured for the sake of the Gospel. Perhaps we seek a cloak, a blanket, a cap to shield against the cold, a Bible, maybe a prayer book or commentary, a volume of poetry or music for the soul. Ultimately, our needs are no different from his, and God's provision for those needs is no less certain. *"Give us this day our daily bread..."*

65. Continues Kingdom Work Until Death

Despite relentless opposition, Paul carried his mission to the very end, confident that the Lord would deliver him to His heavenly kingdom. Church planters, too, are called to persevere in their mission until death, their faith becoming both their catechism and confession (2 Timothy 4:17-18):

"But the Lord stood by me and strengthened me, so that through me the message might be fully proclaimed and all the Gentiles might hear it. So I was delivered from the lion's mouth. The Lord will rescue me from every evil deed and bring me safely into His heavenly kingdom. To Him be the glory forever and ever. Amen."

This is a truth to repeat throughout all your days—a confession to declare against every assault, a prayer to lift up in every trial, and a meditation to hold close until it transforms even the last remnant of the old self. In doing so, you will bring both hope to your own soul and the life-giving power of Gospel hope to a budding Christian community.

66. Values Relationships in the Ministry

Paul's final greetings reflect his deep connections with fellow laborers. The church planter's life and ministry will ultimately be marked by relationships and partnerships for the Lord that will serve to spread the Gospel to the ends of the earth throughout all time (2 Timothy 4:19-22):

> Greet Prisca and Aquila, as well as the household of Onesiphorus.
> Erastus has remained at Corinth, and Trophimus I left sick in Miletus.
> Make every effort to come to me before winter.
> Eubulus sends you greetings, as do Pudens, Linus, Claudia, and all the brothers.
> The Lord be with your spirit. Grace be with you all.

This passage should cause us to recognize the miracle of fishes of loaves, that sharing Christ with one is sharing Him with generations of those who will believe unto everlasting life.

PRAYER

Give us grace, O Lord, to answer readily the call of our Savior Jesus Christ and proclaim to all people the Good News of his salvation, that the whole world may perceive the glory of his marvelous works, who lives and reigns with you and the Holy Spirit, one God, forever and ever. Amen. (Book of Common Prayer, For Missions)

QUESTIONS
FOR REFLECTION AND DISCUSSION

For Chapter Seven

1. How does Paul's single-mindedness in the Gospel charge influence your view of church planting?
2. In what ways can a church planter endure suffering for the sake of the elect?
3. Why is it essential to avoid distractions and meaningless controversies in church planting?
4. How can the practice of restorative discipline shape a church plant's ministry?
5. What role does preaching the Word, in season and out of season, play in the establishment of a new church?
6. How do relationships and fellowship contribute to sustaining a church planter's ministry?

———

SCRIPTURES
FOR MEDITATION AND MEMORIZATION

- "Now it happened in Iconium that they went together to the synagogue of the Jews, and so spoke that a great multitude both of the Jews and of the Greeks believed" (Acts 14:1 NKJV).
- "So, being sent out by the Holy Spirit, they went down to Seleucia, and from there they sailed to Cyprus" (Acts 13:4 NKJV).
- "As they ministered to the Lord and fasted, the Holy Spirit said, 'Now separate to Me Barnabas and Saul for the work to which I have called them'" (Acts 13:2 NKJV).
- "But the word of God grew and multiplied" (Acts 12:24 NKJV).

ADDITIONAL RESOURCES

1. Ferguson, Sinclair B. *The Whole Christ: Legalism, Antinomianism, and Gospel Assurance—Why the Marrow Controversy Still Matters.* Wheaton, IL: Crossway, 2016.
2. Newbigin, Lesslie. *The Gospel in a Pluralist Society.* Grand Rapids: Eerdmans, 1989.
3. Newbigin, Lesslie. *The Household of God: Lectures on the Nature of the Church.* London: SCM Press, 1953.
4. Newton, Phil A. *The Mentoring Church: How Pastors and Congregations Cultivate Leaders.* Grand Rapids: Kregel Ministry, 2017.
5. Tripp, Paul David. *Dangerous Calling: Confronting the Unique Challenges of Pastoral Ministry.* Wheaton, IL: Crossway, 2012.
6. Wright, Christopher J. H. *The Mission of God: Unlocking the Bible's Grand Narrative.* Downers Grove, IL: IVP Academic, 2006.

8

CHURCH PLANTING STRATEGIES
IN THE ACTS OF THE APOSTLES

"And the Lord said to Gideon, 'The people who are with you are too many for Me to give the Midianites into their hands, lest Israel claim glory for itself against Me, saying, "My own hand has saved me." Now therefore, proclaim in the hearing of the people, saying, "Whoever is fearful and afraid, let him turn and depart at once from Mount Gilead."' And twenty-two thousand of the people returned, and ten thousand remained. But the Lord said to Gideon, 'The people are still too many; bring them down to the water, and I will test them for you there.' ... Then the Lord said to Gideon, 'By the three hundred men who lapped I will save you, and deliver the Midianites into your hand. Let all the other people go, every man to his place'" (Judges 7:2-7 NKJV).

We have spent considerable time exploring the life and role of a church planter, drawing upon principles from the pastoral epistles. Now, we turn to the strategies that make church planting effective, asking: "If church planting is among the most effective means to fulfill the Great Commission, how should this work be accomplished?"

CONTEMPORARY STRATEGIES FOR CHURCH PLANTING

The strategies for church planting today echo those of Paul's time, as well as those of Wesley and Whitefield. The primary directive remains, *"Go"* (Matthew 28:19-20). In Acts 13, we see how a prayer meeting concluded with God's clear call to mission:

> "Now in the church at Antioch there were prophets and teachers: Barnabas, Simeon called Niger, Lucius of Cyrene, Manaen (who had been brought up with Herod the tetrarch), and Saul. While they were worshiping the Lord and fasting, the Holy Spirit said, 'Set apart for me Barnabas and Saul for the work to which I have called them.' So after they had fasted and prayed, they placed their hands on them and sent them off" (Acts 13:1-3).

This *sequence* is vital for church planting: *"Now in the church"* (the gathered, covenanted community of believers) signals that the proper origin for church planting is the local assembly of believers. While denominational bodies may initiate a church plant, this local, prayerful foundation is essential. Even when I was sent by a national body to plant a church, it succeeded because a local congregation affirmed, examined, and ultimately sent me.

In this early Antioch church, we see a diversity of Gospel ministers: prophets tasked with proclaiming God's Word until the Scriptures were completed, and teachers ordained and set apart through examination and the laying on of hands (Ephesians 4:11-12). Where a local church lacks this plurality, it is wise to seek help from a larger church body, such as a presbytery, association, or diocese. The next key phrase in this passage is crucial: *"While they were worshiping the Lord and fasting, the Holy Spirit said . . ."* Worship and prayer remain the heart of mission; it is here that God speaks and reveals His will (Psalm 27:4). His call to "go" is unequivocal, but discerning *who* should be sent requires prayerful seeking for both the inner call of the candidate and the outward confirmation from the congregation (Acts 6:3-6).

Out of this seeking, God responds, as He has promised: *"Ask, and it will be given to you; seek, and you will find; knock, and it will be opened to you"* (Matthew 7:7). Speaking as both a teacher of the Word and a church planter, I have found that few callings in the Kingdom of God are as demanding as establishing a new community of believers. Church revitalization, such as Timothy's work in Ephesus (1 Timothy 1:3), ranks close to it. And yet, the most demanding ministries often yield the greatest satisfaction—not in ease or success but in the fulfillment of the mission entrusted to us by Christ (Philippians 4:13).

Thus, Paul, Barnabas, and John Mark began their first missionary journey.

HOW TO PLANT A CHURCH

The biblical-theological principles for church planting remain timeless, as do the responses of those called to plant. Every church planting endeavor should begin with an evangelistic presence in the community, proclaiming Christ in line with Scripture and empowered by the Holy Spirit. In this obedience, the Spirit blesses His own Word and draws people to Christ

(John 6:44; Romans 10:14-15). Reflecting on Paul's journeys, we see a readiness to endure trials, from shipwrecks to imprisonments, always with a commitment to the mission at hand. For Paul, each challenge—be it a snake bite or an arrest—was a divine appointment, a redirection to further the Gospel (2 Corinthians 11:23-28).

This mission-focused perseverance also recalls our Lord's journey to heal Jairus's daughter, during which a woman in desperate need reached out in faith to touch His garment. Jesus's response to her did not detract from His mission; it expanded it (Mark 5:22-34). So, too, for those planting churches, every encounter, even the unexpected, becomes an opportunity to fulfill the Great Commission (Matthew 28:19-20).

Paul assures us that even his imprisonment served to advance the Gospel:

> "Now I want you to know, brothers and sisters, that what has happened to me has actually served to advance the gospel. As a result, it has become clear throughout the whole palace guard and to everyone else that I am in chains for Christ. And because of my chains, most of the brothers and sisters have become confident in the Lord and dare all the more to proclaim the gospel without fear" (Philippians 1:12-14).

Therefore, go. Go with God and preach the Gospel of Jesus Christ. Embrace the ordinary means of church planting listed below and remain open to God's providential interventions that lead to a harvest unforeseen. Plan well. Then, be ready to adjust according to the sovereign surprises that come your way.[1]

CONTEMPORARY EXPRESSIONS OF BIBLICAL CHURCH PLANTING

The following models reflect the practical approaches to church planting, each rooted in the principles found in Scripture:

1 Bible Study Core Group: Often lay-led, a small Bible study group gradually grows into a church.

2 Colonizing: A core group from an established church is sent to form a new church in a different area (Acts 11:22).

3 Evangelist Church Plant: A pastor plants a church with no initial core group, relying solely on a vision and support from a sending body (Acts 16:6-10).

4. Cross-Cultural Church Plant: A cross-cultural church plant is explicitly established to reach a distinct cultural or ethnic group, as exemplified in Acts 10:34-35, where Peter, guided by a vision from God, reaches out to Cornelius, a Gentile, with the Gospel: *"In truth, I perceive that God shows no partiality. But in every nation, whoever fears Him and works righteousness is accepted by Him."* This approach is not driven by demographic considerations or institutional representation but by a genuine, Spirit-given burden to share Christ across cultural boundaries.

In this sense, cross-cultural church planting resembles chaplaincy, where the chaplain fully identifies with the people they serve. Similarly, in cross-cultural ministry, the church planter enters the life and experiences of the targeted group, establishing a community of Christ through Word, Sacrament, and Prayer, with a heart to truly understand and care for those they serve. The goal is not simply to diversify but to minister authentically from within the cultural context of those God has burdened us to reach.

To say, *"We need to plant churches to reach Hispanic peoples because our denomination lacks Hispanic representation"* may have good intentions, but it falls short of God's vision for mission. Our calling is not about expanding a denominational footprint or fulfilling representation metrics. Rather, it is about the Gospel itself—the proclamation of Christ in word and deed to those who have not yet heard or embraced the good news. We are called to fulfill the trans-generational discipleship mandate given by our Lord, bearing a Christ-centered love that crosses cultural lines out of an actual burden for the salvation and sanctification of all people.

5 Re-Plant: A struggling church is revitalized with a new church planter who leads and renews the congregation.

These models offer practical pathways to church planting, but to understand the biblical foundation, we turn to the Book of Acts, where the early Church provides a divinely inspired framework.

A SUMMARY OF BIBLICAL STRATEGIES IN ACTS FOR CHURCH PLANTING

We review what we have gleaned.

The Book of Acts offers many strategies aligned with Gospel expansion, each rooted in prayer and dependence on God's power.[2] Key strategies include:

1 Prayer Meetings: Before Pentecost, the disciples gathered for prayer, seeking guidance and power from God (Acts 1:14). Worship and prayer are essential for discerning God's will. We have stated this repeatedly, perhaps to the point of frustration to the reader. Yet, the Bible does not hesitate to repeat the most critical factors in the Great Commission and the Christian life.

2 Evangelistic Preaching: Peter's sermon at Pentecost led to 3,000 baptisms (Acts 2:41-47). Church planting must start with preaching the Gospel.

3 Local Church Renewal: As the apostles focused on prayer and teaching, the Church grew in strength and numbers (Acts 6:1-7).

4 Persecution: The scattering of believers due to persecution led to the spread of the Gospel (Acts 8:1-4). Be alert to the Lord's work, often disguised as men's work. Pioneers heading westward in the 19th century became a time of revival for those Methodist, Baptist, and Lutheran pastors who followed. Where are the wagon trains in your area? What are they? Why? Population movement is one of the most overlooked but vital variables in identifying an area crying out for the Gospel. Unsettledness equals Gospel ministry and kingdom indicators.

5 Human Migration and Lay-Led Missionary Work: Ordinary believers shared the Gospel, forming new congregations (Acts 8:4). The dispersion of believers is an ordinary way that churches are planted. Human migration is a Biblical pathway to church planting, whether by political or economic causes, natural disasters, work (i.e., transfers), military service, or even persecution.

6 Breaking Down Divisions: Peter's vision and encounter with Cornelius exemplify the Gospel's power to transcend cultural barriers (Acts 10:34-35).

These strategies remind us that church planting depends on divine guidance, prayer, and unwavering obedience to the Great Commission.

MOVING FORWARD

The strategies revealed in Acts demonstrate the necessity of relying on God's power and the faithful proclamation of the

Gospel. Whether through organized evangelism, persecution, or the growth of new believers, church planting is not a mere human endeavor but a divine mission. By examining these biblical examples alongside contemporary methods, we gain a framework for fulfilling the Great Commission in our generation.

PRAYER

Keep, O Lord, Your household, the Church, in Your steadfast faith and love, that through Your grace we may proclaim Your truth with boldness and minister Your justice with compassion for the sake of our Savior Jesus Christ, who lives and reigns with You and the Holy Spirit, one God, now and forever. Amen. (Book of Common Prayer, for Missions)

QUESTIONS
FOR REFLECTION AND DISCUSSION

For Chapter Eight

1 What role does the local church play in the process of church planting, and why is it crucial that this calling emerges from the "gathered, covenanted community" rather than solely from a higher denominational authority? Reflect on Acts 13:1-3 and consider how the Antioch model informs our understanding of local church support and affirmation in sending missionaries.

2 How does the call to "go" in the Great Commission (Matthew 28:19-20) challenge each of us, not only to obedience but to trust in God's provision and timing for His mission? In what ways does this command reorient our lives toward a deeper dependence on God's power and guidance?

3 In the book of Acts, prayer and fasting are foundational to church planting efforts. How do these disciplines prepare a church and its leaders to discern God's will? Reflect on Acts 1:14 and Acts 13:2-3 and consider how our own ministries might benefit from a renewal of these spiritual practices.

4 Paul's experiences in church planting often involved hardship and unexpected "redirections" from God, such as shipwrecks or imprisonment. How might we view obstacles in our ministry as potential "divine appointments"? Consider Philippians 1:12-14, reflecting on how even adversity can become a means of Gospel advancement.

5 How do contemporary church planting methods, like core group Bible studies or cross-cultural church plants, connect with the strategies found in Acts? Explore how these methods might be adapted to meet the needs of diverse communities while remaining faithful to biblical principles.

6 Reflecting on the phrase "sovereign surprises," how can we stay open to God's unforeseen interventions in our ministry plans? In what ways does such openness not only further the mission but deepen our faith and reliance on God, reinforcing our commitment to the Great Commission?

SCRIPTURES
FOR MEDITATION AND MEMORIZATION

- "For the Son of Man has come to seek and to save that which was lost" (Luke 19:10 NKJV).
- "A sower went out to sow his seed. And as he sowed, some fell by the wayside; and it was trampled down, and the birds of the air devoured it. Some fell on rock; and as soon as it sprang up, it withered away because it lacked moisture. And some fell among thorns, and the thorns sprang up with it and choked it. But others fell on good ground, sprang up, and yielded a crop a hundredfold." When He had said these things He cried, 'He who has ears to hear, let him hear!'" (Luke 8:5-8 NKJV).
- "I am a debtor both to Greeks and to barbarians, both to wise and to unwise" (Romans 1:14 NKJV).
- "And they continued steadfastly in the apostles' doctrine and fellowship, in the breaking of bread, and in prayers" (Acts 2:42 NKJV).

ADDITIONAL RESOURCES

1. Allen, Roland. *Missionary Methods: St. Paul's or Ours?* Grand Rapids: Eerdmans, 1962.
2. Bosch, David J. *Transforming Mission: Paradigm Shifts in Theology of Mission.* Maryknoll, NY: Orbis Books, 1991.
3. Frost, Michael. *The Shaping of Things to Come: Innovation and Mission for the 21st-Century Church.* Peabody, MA: Hendrickson Publishers, 2003.
4. Glasser, Arthur F. *Announcing the Kingdom: The Story of God's Mission in the Bible.* Grand Rapids, MI: Baker Academic, 2003.
5. Guder, Darrell L. *Missional Church: A Vision for the Sending of the Church in North America.* Grand Rapids, MI: Eerdmans, 1998.
6. McGavran, Donald A. *Understanding Church Growth.* 3rd ed. Grand Rapids, MI: Eerdmans, 1990.
7. Ott, Craig, and Gene Wilson. *Global Church Planting: Biblical Principles and Best Practices for*

Multiplication. Grand Rapids, MI: Baker Academic, 2011.

8. Van Engen, Charles. "Toward a Theology of Mission: Understanding God's Mission." *Missiology: An International Review* 21, no. 4 (1993): 473-492.

9. Woodward, J.R. *Creating a Missional Culture: Equipping the Church for the Sake of the World*. Downers Grove, IL: InterVarsity Press, 2012.

———

9
PREPARING THE CHURCH PLANTING PLAN

"Commit your works to the Lord, and your thoughts will be established" (Proverbs 16:3 NKJV).

"For which of you, intending to build a tower, does not sit down first and count the cost, whether he has enough to finish it—lest, after he has laid the foundation, and is not able to finish, all who see it begin to mock him, saying, 'This man began to build and was not able to finish,'" (Luke 14:28-30 NKJV)?

The journey into church planting demands practical application of the theology and biblical principles we've studied. A well-prepared plan ensures the church planter has a solid theological foundation and a workable, organized strategy. You can examine a church planting plan, a vision and mission plan, and find a template in the appendices of this book.

THE CHURCH PLANTING PLAN: COMPONENTS

1. The Narrative: The narrative leads to the burden, the values, vision, mission, philosophy of ministry, and, quite possibly, even the strategic steps. The narrative is not something you make up as you go. The narrative is the studied result of prayerful investigation: spiritually, demographically (simply put, people, people movement, human activity in the community), and sociologically (e.g., patterns in family life, education, crime, church attendance). Start with a detailed narrative, including assumptions gathered beforehand, such as demographic data about the community. Demographic insights can come from online resources or dedicated ministries that provide an area's ministry area profiles (MAP). Yet, shall we plant churches on demographic studies alone? God forbid. Prayer and fasting should also accompany data analysis, allowing spiritual discernment to *lead t*he planning process. Sometimes, a burden for human beings will direct you to a rural area that is not as demographically attractive but is more in need of a Gospel community. Let burden guide you first and foremost. All other resources are tools to sharpen the strategic arrows of the mission. They cannot constitute the mission itself.

Another concern with demographic studies: The consultants will rarely look for spiritual trends across time. We have found that there are areas where churches have been difficult to establish because of an apparent demonic hold on the region, often the consequence of an entrance created by great sin. The older Southern port cities of North America (e.g., New Orleans) where slave trading was active is a possible example. Because of the buying and selling of human beings, there existed a veritable "open border" for nefarious, bad spiritual actors. The Emancipation Proclamation did not instantly bind the demons. There may still be demonic strongholds. In such cases, evil shall not withstand the coming of the Kingdom of God. But approaching it from demographic studies alone will not dislodge these fallen angels. Deep roots in a Biblical and theological framework might suffer attack from the ensconced diabolical forces. Still, they cannot stop the preaching of the cross (i.e., the crucified, risen, ascended, ruling, and coming Jesus Christ being *the* message).

While the narrative should follow the headings below (burden, values, vision, mission, philosophy of ministry, and steps), it should be presented most personally. Thus, *don't tell. Show.* Don't give demographic figures or sociological trends of people movement statistics (footnote them, yes) but show the reader (presumably, those who will support the work with prayer and finances, as well as members of a prospective core group). If an area is experiencing growth, you might express this by starting the narrative: "Brett and Samantha never dreamed they would live in Kansas City. But two years into his first job after college, with an engineering firm, Brett was transferred to Overland Park, Kansas, the principle suburban city outside of KC." Write a narrative about the profile of the family you envision in your study.

2. Assumptions and Foundations Before writing, consider:

- **Prayer**: Seeking God's guidance. What is the anchor Scriptural passage that is guiding you in prayer? Mine was always the same: "And let the beauty of the LORD our God be upon us, And establish the work of our hands for us; Yes, establish the work of our hands" (Psalm 90:17).
- **Church Planter Assessment**: Including your wife and a solid support network. It may be redundant

to state that the church planter cannot advance to the field without the approbation of others who have examined him, but it cannot be overemphasized.
- **Community Assessment**: Surveying the field involves a prayerful study of spiritual, sociological, and demographic trends in a given area (read sociology and demographics through prayer and attention to spiritual warfare, not merely as a marketing exercise).

3. Burden, Values, and Vision: Present the burden for the area, articulating the spiritual or physical need that the church plant will address. Identify core values that will guide the ministry, even though not exhaustive. Lastly, paint a vision—a concise depiction of how the community will look when that burden is lifted.

- **Naming the Church:** Choose a church name that reflects the church's mission, such as how Old Testament names mirrored events or divine interventions. **The name of a respective Christian community should reflect the vision that lifts the burden.** Hope, Redeemer, and Good Shepherd are examples of this naming protocol.
  - Even a geographical name (Fairhope Reformed Church) should connect the community of believers to the need for this church in the larger community).

5. Mission and Philosophy of Ministry Write a clear mission statement explaining how the church will meet the vision through its ministry. Include critical aspects of your philosophy of ministry: outreach, worship, preaching, discipleship, missions, and mercy.

6. Strategic Plans Outline both long-term and short-term goals. Your strategic plan should include staffing projections, officer training plans, and event planning, such as Dedication Sunday.

Before the dawn of digital project planning, I used sticky notes on my bedroom wall (which also served as my office) to move through the project milestones. I began with a wall entire of sticky notes. I concluded with a Dedication Sunday where we laid hands on elders and deacons, and I was installed as the pastor. There should never be a moment when you do not know your place in the project. You could use the suggested division in this volume (surveying the land, planting, cultivating, harvesting) to add specific tasks to each phase, from finding a place to begin preaching and conducting worship services (e.g., in your living room on a Sunday evening) to establishing treasury protocols and banking, to meeting with community leaders and other pastors, all the way to Dedication Sunday. If you are part of a denomination, you will undoubtedly enjoy the blessings of a connectional church in this area.

A BIBLICAL VISION AND MISSION

"I am the light of the world. He who follows Me shall not walk in darkness, but have the light of life." (John 8:12 NKJV)

1 Identifying the Burden

Begin by discerning the burden—a concern that reflects not just personal or communal interest but God's own burden as revealed in Scripture. This burden should connect deeply with the needs of your context, such as fostering healing and new life through governance, Christian education, or pastoral ministry, for instance, in response to specific challenges like those faced by Mother Emanuel AME Church in the aftermath of tragedy.

2 Values

Identify the core convictions that will guide your response to this burden. These values should be deeply rooted in a theological understanding, reflecting God's character and your church community's unique needs.

3 Vision

Develop a clear vision statement, a concise expression of the desired transformation in response to the identified burden. The vision should capture a picture of restoration and growth that reflects God's redemptive purpose for your context.

4 Mission

Articulate your mission, which addresses the practical steps and theological commitments necessary to fulfill the vision. The mission is the "how"—the actions, principles, and spiritual practices that will lead the church in lifting the identified burden.

5 Philosophy of Ministry

Outline your philosophy of ministry, an abbreviated statement of the biblical approach that will undergird your efforts. This approach emphasizes foundational Christian practices such as personal evangelism, expository preaching, and hospitality, creating an authentic and welcoming church in, for example, an urban area where anonymity and isolation may abound.

6 Strategies

Define the concrete strategies or steps that will bring the mission to life. These actionable steps should be specific, achievable, and aligned with your overall mission and vision, ensuring that the church remains focused and purposeful in its work.

Example of a Vision and Mission Plan

Below is an example illustrating how a burden gives rise to a values-based vision and mission, along with a philosophy of ministry that is both biblical and practical. This plan serves as a model, with additional examples for local churches available in Appendix 1. This statement begins with a summary notice concerning the motto, anchor verse, and teaching vision. The vision and mission components then follow.

The D. James Kennedy Institute of Reformed Leadership
Vision and Mission Statement
First Things

- **Motto:** *Excellence in all things and all things for Christ*
- **Anchor Verse:** *"And you shall know the truth, and the truth shall make you free"* (John 8:32 NKJV).
- **Vision of Teaching:**

"The end then of Learning is to repair the ruins of our first Parents by regaining to know God aright, and out of that knowledge to love Him, to imitate Him, to be like Him, as we may the nearest by possessing our souls of true virtue, which being united to the heavenly grace of faith makes up the highest perfection." —John Milton, *On Education* (1644)

A vision and mission statement must express the identity and purpose of the ministry, emerging from God's burden, values, vision, mission, and a Christ-centered philosophy of ministry.

Burden

The D. James Kennedy Institute operates with a burden for the biblical revelation of spiritual darkness and the need for cultural redemption, seeking to free humanity from enslavement to the devil's domain.

Ephesians 6:12 NKJV: *"For we do not wrestle against flesh and blood, but against principalities, against powers, against the rulers of the darkness of this age, against spiritual hosts of wickedness in the heavenly places."*

Values

Rooted in Scripture and the Great Commission, the Institute's work is guided by Reformed theological principles that are central to its mission.

Hebrews 4:14 NKJV: *"Seeing then that we have a great High Priest who has passed through the heavens, Jesus the Son of God, let us hold fast our confession."*

Vision

The Institute seeks to impart transformative truths grounded in the Gospel, equipping believers to live faithfully under the Lordship of Christ.

John 8:31-32 NKJV: *"If you abide in My word, you are My disciples indeed. And you shall know the truth, and the truth shall make you free."*

Mission

Our mission is fulfilled through Research, Writing, and Resource Development to serve the Church by:

- **Teaching**: Presenting Gospel truths that resonate with the Reformed faith and public theology.
- **Equipping**: Nurturing pastoral leaders to guide and develop Christ's flock.

Ephesians 6:13 NKJV: *"Therefore take up the whole armor of God, that you may be able to withstand in the evil day, and having done all, to stand."*

Philosophy of Ministry

Following the motto, *"Excellence in all things and all things for Christ,"* the Institute emphasizes a God-glorifying standard that reflects the Cultural Mandate (Genesis 1:26-28), the Great Commandment (Matthew 22:35-40), and the Great Commission (Matthew 28:19-20).

Matthew 5:16 NKJV: *"Let your light so shine before men, that they may see your good works and glorify your Father in heaven."*

Our high and privileged calling is to do the will of God in the power of God for the glory of God.—James I. Packer[1]

QUESTIONS
FOR REFLECTION AND DISCUSSION

FOR CHAPTER NINE

1. How does demographic data inform church planting without overshadowing the spiritual discernment necessary for successful ministry?
2. What are the essential nonnegotiable values that guide your ministry, and how do they shape your church plant?
3. How does your mission align with the Great Commission in practical terms?
4. Why is the name of a church more than just a label? How can it shape community perception and vision?
5. What are the greatest challenges in balancing long-term vision and short-term practical goals in church planting?
6. In what ways can officer training and leadership

development ensure sustainability for the future of the church plant?

———

SCRIPTURES
FOR MEDITATION & MEMORIZATION

- "And this gospel of the kingdom will be preached in all the world as a witness to all the nations, and then the end will come" (Matthew 24:14 NKJV).
- "But grow in the grace and knowledge of our Lord and Savior Jesus Christ. To Him be the glory both now and forever. Amen" (2 Peter 3:18 NKJV).
- "I, therefore, the prisoner of the Lord, beseech you to walk worthy of the calling with which you were called, with all lowliness and gentleness, with longsuffering, bearing with one another in love, endeavoring to keep the unity of the Spirit in the bond of peace. There is one body and one Spirit, just as you were called in one hope of your calling; one Lord, one faith, one baptism" (Ephesians 4:1-5 NKJV).
- "And let us not grow weary while doing good, for in due season we shall reap if we do not lose heart" (Galatians 6:9 NKJV).

ADDITIONAL RESOURCES

1. Barnes, M. Craig. *The Pastor as Minor Poet: Texts and Subtexts in the Ministerial Life.* Grand Rapids, MI: Eerdmans, 2008.
2. Bolman, Lee G., and Terrence E. Deal. *Reframing Organizations: Artistry, Choice, and Leadership.* 5th ed. San Francisco, CA: Jossey-Bass, 2017.
3. Conn, Harvie M. *Eternal Word and Changing Worlds: Theology, Anthropology, and Mission in Trialogue.* Grand Rapids, MI: Zondervan, 1984.
4. Fitch, David E. *Faithful Presence: Seven Disciplines That Shape the Church for Mission.* Downers Grove, IL: InterVarsity Press, 2016.
5. Green, Chris. *Sanctifying Interpretation: Vocation, Holiness, and Scripture in a Post-Christian World.* Waco, TX: Baylor University Press, 2020.
6. Guder, Darrell L., ed. *Missional Church: A Vision for the Sending of the Church in North America.* Grand Rapids, MI: Eerdmans, 1998.

7. Hunter, George G. *The Celtic Way of Evangelism: How Christianity Can Reach the West... Again.* Nashville, TN: Abingdon Press, 2000.
8. Roxburgh, Alan J. *Missional: Joining God in the Neighborhood.* Grand Rapids, MI: Baker Books, 2011.
9. Roxburgh, Alan J., and M. Scott Boren. *Introducing the Missional Church: What It Is, Why It Matters, How to Become One.* Grand Rapids, MI: Baker Books, 2009.

10

MISCELLANEOUS CONCERNS
FAITH, FAMILY, AND THE PREPONDERANT SINS

"Seek first the kingdom of God and His righteousness, and all these things shall be added to you" (Matthew 6:33 NKJV).

The final chapter is not here because these issues are less critical—rather, they hold the ultimate place, much like the last figure in a procession signifies the leader. If your faith, family, or diligence in guarding against the snares of the devil falter, then the guidance of this book falls short. Thus, we devote a few solemn words to these categories, trusting that brevity reflects gravity. This chapter is a call for alertness in areas where many Christian shepherds and church planters have faced downfall. Faith, family, and vigilance against sin are interconnected, and weakness in one area inevitably spills over into the others.

FAITH

The starting point is your own faith and personal devotion to Jesus Christ. The church planter faces a unique danger: his soul is at risk precisely because of the mission field. This may seem paradoxical, but the frontlines of kingdom work are a prime environment for spiritual attack.

A minister's calling is his sanctification. Paul underscores this connection when he warns Timothy:

> "Neglect not the gift that is in thee, which was given thee by prophecy, with the laying on of the hands of the presbytery. Meditate upon these things; give thyself wholly to them; that thy profiting may appear to all. Take heed unto thyself, and unto the doctrine; continue in them; for in doing this thou shalt both save thyself and them that hear thee" (1 Timothy 4:14-16 KJV).

Paul's charge—"Neglect not the gift," "Meditate," "give thyself wholly," "take heed to thyself, and unto the doctrine," and "continue in them"—reveals the vital link between the pastor's ministry and his own spiritual life. Paul isn't advocating clerical elitism; rather, he recognizes the unique calling of the pastor, who bears responsibility for feeding the flock with the Word, Sacraments, and communal prayer. Ordinarily, a pastor fulfills this role weekly, but the church planter's context is different, engaged as he is in an unsettled missionary work. His task is to "put in order the things that remain," as Paul instructed Titus. Therefore, he must consciously cultivate his faith and the spiritual health of his household.

One way to guard against spiritual neglect is to structure the church planter's life as if he were in a settled pastorate.

This means committing to sermon preparation, gathering people for prayer, and studying the Scriptures as regularly as possible. For example, consider using a church calendar and lectionary to guide your sermons and devotionals, following the life of Jesus throughout the year. This approach fosters continuity in teaching and discipleship, even in the pioneering setting of church planting.

We strongly recommend writing a weekly sermon manuscript. While not advocating that you read it verbatim in your gatherings, the discipline of writing out your thoughts clarifies your message and promotes personal growth. Read the manuscript to your family or a trusted circle, seeking feedback on the content and the spiritual impact. Is the Gospel presented? Does the message communicate hope, truth, and transformation?

In sum, act as though you already have a congregation gathered regularly. This discipline will help you live out the five instructions from Paul—neglect not the gift, meditate, give yourself wholly, take heed, and continue in the doctrine—ensuring you "save both yourself and them that hear thee."

FAMILY

No man is ultimately more effective in public ministry than he is in private ministry to his family. This truth applies to all pastors, but church planting presents unique challenges.

The church planter's wife is not a co-pastor or "assistant minister." Her primary role is to care for her husband and their home, enabling him to serve others. My wife once answered a pulpit committee member who asked about her role: "I take care of him so that he can take care of you." Her response is both descriptive and prescriptive. While the church planter's wife may naturally be more visible due to the intimate nature of church planting, her ministry within the home remains foundational.

Church planting frequently requires hospitality—often in the pastor's own home. If the pastor's wife is uncomfortable with hosting, hospitality can be extended in other ways, yet the couple must anticipate the visibility and accessibility that accompany their roles. Furthermore, the children of church planters are likewise thrust into a "fishbowl" environment, watched closely by the surrounding community. But we might amend that image, recalling that the pastoral family often feels more like they are in a "lion's den" due to spiritual attacks. Such pressures underscore the importance of gathering together as a family in the Word, seeking God's strength and protection. "Cotter's Saturday night" worship binds the family together in the Lord's grace, guarding them against the forces that seek to disrupt or even destroy.

In Christ, you will find that the trials faced as a family can deepen your love, strengthen your resolve, and prepare you for the work to come. If the family approaches this ministry in humility and reliance on God, then the trials of church planting become how the Lord refines and strengthens them.

SPIRITUAL DANGERS AND PREPONDERANT SINS

All Christians are susceptible to the sins of the flesh, yet the consequences are particularly weighty for pastors. Church planting is a spiritually demanding work, often involving stages that unfold over long, unpredictable timelines: selecting a site, evangelizing, enfolding members into fellowship, and discipling them. Each stage presents unique challenges, and these hardships can open the door to discouragement, exhaustion, and even spiritual depression. In these weakened states, the sins of the flesh—whether gluttony, lust, anger, or envy—may appeal as temporary reliefs or distractions. The pastor must remain vigilant, aware that the world, the flesh, and the devil are eager to exploit any vulnerability.

The antidote is Gospel-centered living, grounded in a deep, personal identification with the cross. The cross-shaped life sees trials not as obstacles but as opportunities for growth. The very trials meant to hinder us are transformed into means of grace. Thus, when expectations fall short, remember that disappointment is a natural response—but bring that disappointment to the One who is sovereign over all.

EMBRACING THE BATTLE

The task of church planting is not merely a human endeavor but a spiritual battle. We must keep in mind the ultimate triumph revealed in Revelation 12:1-12, a passage that echoes through every age and every planting of the Gospel:

> "Now war arose in heaven...And the great dragon was thrown down...And they have conquered him by the blood of the Lamb and by the word of their testimony, for they loved not their lives even unto death...the devil has come down to you in great wrath, because he knows that his time is short" (Revelation 12:1-12 ESV).

The birth, death, and resurrection of Jesus mark Satan's defeat. Though he wars against us, our victory is assured. Christ has overcome, and in Him, we overcome. The reality of church planting is the reality of spiritual opposition, yet also of inevitable triumph in Christ.

In that light, any work we do for the Kingdom, even when met with disappointment and delay, is secure in Christ.

"But I would ye should understand, brethren, that the things which happened unto me have fallen out rather unto the furtherance of the gospel" (Philippians 1:12 KJV).

OUR ETERNAL VISION

In all our labors, we look toward a glory that surpasses this life:

"For what is our hope, or joy, or crown of rejoicing? Is it not even you in the presence of our Lord Jesus Christ at His coming? For you are our glory and joy" (1 Thessalonians 2:19-20 NKJV).

We plant churches in obedience to Christ's Great Commission and labor to see souls gathered safely into His Kingdom. This vision transcending this world is our "glory and joy."

PRAYER

Lord of the Harvest, As You sent Your Son, our Savior Jesus Christ, to establish His New Covenant Church to fulfill Your revealed vision for a New Heaven and a New Earth, call and send Your New Testament evangelists endued with power from on high to obediently proclaim repentance and faith to all people through Jesus Christ our Lord. Amen.

CLASS PROJECT
A CHURCH PLANTING PLAN

Old Testament: Proverbs 2:3-6

"Yes, if you cry out for discernment, and lift up your voice for understanding, if you seek her as silver, and search for her as for hidden treasures; then you will understand the fear of the Lord, and find the knowledge of God. For the Lord gives wisdom; from His mouth come knowledge and understanding" (Proverbs 2:3-6 NKJV).

"Be diligent to present yourself approved to God, a worker who does not need to be ashamed, rightly dividing the word of truth" (2 Timothy 2:15 NKJV).

I have included this section in service to Christian higher education, mainly theological higher education and vocational training in the West. However, the truths and the training assignment can be used, with contextual adjustments, anywhere and anytime.

THE ASSIGNMENT

Students will create a church planting plan for a chosen location, which includes:

Study the demographics (what does the data suggest to you as a pastor? What spiritual dynamics are present? What hinders? What helps?

Write a narrative of no more than twelve pages describing the family or household you seek to reach. Follow the pattern below. In other words, you should personalize your church planting plan for a specific family or individual. The burden, values, vision, mission, and philosophy of ministry provide a framework for assessing the fallen condition of the community and applying the Gospel to these people. A well-written church planting narrative will likely also give a name for the church plant. Rather than mimicking others, allow the name and identity of the church plant to arise from what God is doing in this community.

THE VISION AND MISSION FACTORS

Each of these factors in a vision and mission plan is connected. The thoughtful response to these questions is contextualized by the church planting narrative and guided by Scripture and the Gospel story (Creation, Fall, Redemption, Consummation). In this way, the daily work of the church planter is guided and guarded by these immovable stakes. From this, a foundation is laid. A superstructure is erected. A community of the Holy Spirit is born, established, and prayerfully will be in place when Christ comes again. This is our prayer:

> "Let your work be shown to your servants, and your glorious power to their children. Let the favor of the Lord our God be

upon us, and establish the work of our hands upon us; yes, establish the work of our hands!" (Psalm 90:16–17, ESV)

We have suggested questions to help you formulate the vision and mission plan. These are designed to support your efforts, not to restrain your thoughts.

QUESTIONS FOR A VISION AND MISSION PLAN

Burden: What spiritual need does this plant address? This pervasive vestige of the fall is present in the community and is understood and carefully stated after completing the church planting narrative. We are broken by the pain of ___ and believe that a new covenanted community of Jesus Christ can bring healing now and through the generations.

Values: What are the core guiding principles? These are not the only prominent features. Your denomination, but the highlighted values given the burden in the church planting narrative. As we seek to establish a covenanted community of Christ obediently, our values include but are not limited to _, _, and _.

Vision: What will this community look like when transformed by the Gospel? How does the vision lift the burden? We are a covenanted community of our Lord Jesus Christ bringing _ to heal ____.

Mission: How do we move towards the vision? We seek the Vision of this local community of disciples of Jesus Christ by _____.

Philosophy of Ministry: How will you gather, grow, and send forth strong disciples of Jesus Christ?

We will gather, grow, and send forth strong disciples of Jesus Christ by ___.

Strategic Response: What observable, measurable steps must be taken to activate the mission and help us move to the vision? We want our covenanted community to be grounded in the Biblical vision and mission of our Lord Jesus Christ. With faith in His plans, we humbly submit our work to Him and pray that He will establish the work of our hands. Our strategy for grounding and growth includes:

SURVEYING THE LAND:

1. Why must you go to this place?

2. What are the invisible spiritual issues involved that are visible in material examples?

3. Where has this community been spiritually and materially? Where do they seem to be going?

4. Seek God in prayer with other ministers and lay leaders in the local church and, if relevant, the host church or a nearby congregation. What is the Lord saying through His Word and in observing His providence (not anticipating, but noting what He has already done)? Prepare the Church Planting Mission Plan with a strong narrative that logically leads to the church plant.

TILLING THE SOIL:

1. Pastor's annual planning and weekly preparation

2. Weekly preaching services in a home.

3. Weekly Men's Bible Study in a public place, e.g., a coffee shop (women's study to follow in season 2).

PLANTING THE SEED:

1. Follow the Church Year to highlight the life of Christ and preach through a book of the Bible presented in a respective lectionary or plan.

2. Go through the Acts of the Apostles or the Gospel of John with men. Equip the men to share Christ in their lives. Enfold more men into the work. Direct these men to Sunday night "sacred assembly," e.g., in your home.

Reaping the Harvest:

1. Establish a goal (with a recognizable watershed moment indicating it is time) for training for lay leadership (e.g., elder and deacon).

2. Establish a goal (and signs for readiness) for particularization (ordination of local lay leadership).

QUESTIONS
FOR REFLECTION AND DISCUSSION

For Chapter Ten

1. How can a church planter balance the spiritual needs of the church with the emotional and relational needs of his family?
2. In what ways does ambiguity in church planting challenge a family's faith, and how can they prepare for it?
3. How can spiritual disciplines counteract the discouragement or pride that often comes with church planting?
4. What unique challenges do evangelist-driven church plants face, and how can they safeguard against the dangers of isolation?
5. Why is it critical for a church plant to have a clear vision from the beginning, and how should this be communicated to the core group?
6. How can church planters avoid the pitfalls of

leadership issues, such as vision hijacking or reluctance to relinquish control?

———

SCRIPTURES
FOR MEDITATION & MEMORIZATION

- "So those who received his word were baptized; and that day about three thousand souls were added to them" (Acts 2:41 NKJV).
- "But you shall receive power when the Holy Spirit has come upon you; and you shall be witnesses to Me in Jerusalem, and in all Judea and Samaria, and to the end of the earth" (Acts 1:8 NKJV).
- "Then all the tax collectors and the sinners drew near to Him to hear Him. And the Pharisees and scribes complained, saying, 'This Man receives sinners and eats with them.' So He spoke this parable to them, saying: 'What man of you, having a hundred sheep, if he loses one of them, does not leave the ninety-nine in the wilderness, and go after the one which is lost until he finds it? And when he has found it, he lays it on his shoulders, rejoicing'" (Luke 15:1-5 NKJV).
- "Then the master said to the servant, 'Go out into the highways and hedges, and compel them to

come in, that my house may be filled'" (Luke 14:23 NKJV).

ADDITIONAL RESOURCES

1. Cole, Neil. *Organic Church: Growing Faith Where Life Happens.* San Francisco: Jossey-Bass, 2005.
2. Hirsch, Alan. *The Forgotten Ways: Reactivating the Missional Church.* Grand Rapids, MI: Brazos Press, 2009.
3. Frost, Michael. *The Road to Missional: Journey to the Center of the Church.* Grand Rapids, MI: Baker Books, 2011.
4. Heath, Chip, and Dan Heath. *Switch: How to Change Things When Change Is Hard.* New York: Crown Business, 2010.
5. Murray, Stuart. *Planting Churches in the 21st Century: A Guide for Those Who Want Fresh Perspectives and New Ideas for Creating Congregations.* Scottdale, PA: Herald Press, 2010.
6. Van Gelder, Craig, and Dwight J. Zscheile. *The Missional Church in Perspective: Mapping Trends and Shaping the Conversation.* Grand Rapids, MI: Baker Academic, 2011.

ADDITIONAL RESOURCES

NOTES

1. THE ESSENCE OF CHURCH PLANTING

1. See George Eldon Ladd and D. A. Hagner, *A Theology of the New Testament* (Eerdmans Publishing Company, 1993).

4. THE PORTRAIT OF THE CHURCH PLANTER

1. Charles Haddon Spurgeon, *The New Park Street Pulpit: Sermons Preached and Revised by C.H. Spurgeon During the Year 1855* (London: Passmore & Alabaster, 1856), 198.
2. James Bannerman, *The Church of Christ: A Treatise on the Nature, Powers, Ordinances, Discipline, and Government of the Christian Church*, vol. 1 (Edinburgh: T&T Clark, 1868), 3.

5. THE PORTRAIT OF THE CHURCH PLANTER

1. George W. Knight, *The Pastoral Epistles: A Commentary on the Greek Text*, New International Greek Testament Commentary (Grand Rapids, MI; Carlisle, England: W.B. Eerdmans; Paternoster Press, 1992), 182.
2. "What follows may be a fragment of an early Christian hymn or creedal confession, composed of three balanced couplets." R. C. Sproul, ed., *The Reformation Study Bible: English Standard Version (2015 Edition)* (Orlando, FL: Reformation Trust, 2015), 2159.
3. σῶμα sōma; of unc. or.; *a body*:—bodies(11), body(128), personal(1), slaves(1), substance(1).

    Robert L. Thomas, *New American Standard Hebrew-Aramaic and Greek Dictionaries: Updated Edition* (Anaheim: Foundation Publications, Inc., 1998).
4. Bannerman, *The Church of Christ*, volume 1, 97.
5. John R. W. Stott, *The Preacher's Portrait: Five New Testament Word Studies* (Langham Preaching Resources, 2016).
6. Stott, *Preacher's Portrait*, v.
7. John Bunyan, *The Pilgrim's Progress from This World to That Which Is to Come, Delivered under the Similitude of a Dream* (London: Nathaniel Ponder, 1678).

7. THE PORTRAIT OF THE CHURCH PLANTER

1. William Hendriksen, *More Than Conquerors: An Interpretation of the Book of Revelation* (Baker Books, 1998).
2. The references here are:v [1] *The New King James Version* (Nashville: Thomas Nelson, 1982), 2 Ti 3:8–9.

    [2] A. F. Walls, "Jannes and Jambres," in *New Bible Dictionary*, ed. D. R. W. Wood et al. (Leicester, England; Downers Grove, IL: InterVarsity Press, 1996), 543.

    [3] *Christian Standard Bible* (Nashville, TN: Holman Bible Publishers, 2020), 2 Ti 3:7–10.

    [4] Brian Simmons, trans., *The Passion Translation* (BroadStreet Publishing, 2017), 2 Ti 3:7–8.
3. "Paul was not married at the time of his ministry (see 1 Cor. 7:7; 9:5; it is impossible to know whether he was previously married or not)." The ESV Study Bible, p 2544
4. "'Paul: Apostle of the Heart Set Free' is a book by F. F. Bruce, published in 1977 by Eerdmans in Grand Rapids" (from a "summary" in Logos).
5. For interpretation of this verse consider the careful scholarship of George W. Knight III: (**4:13**, p 467) "Paul also wants Timothy to bring "the books." βιβλίον (NT 34x, Pl.* 2x: Gal. 3:10) "is the most common word for the 'roll of a book,' a 'book,' or a 'writing' in the *koine*" (G. Schrenk, *TDNT* I, 617). In both the LXX and the NT it is used of any writing in general (e.g., Dt. 24:1, 3; Mk. 10:4; Mt. 19:7) and to refer to individual OT writings (e.g., 1 Ch. 27:24; cf. the related word βίβλοι in Dan. 9:2), particularly as "a solemn expression for the Book of the Law" (U. Becker, *NIDNTT* I, 243, referring to Dt. 28:58; Jos. 1:8; so also in Josephus [Schrenk, 617, n. 9]). Thus in the NT it is used in the expressions "the book of the prophet Isaiah" (Lk. 4:17) and "the book of the law" (Gal. 3:10) and by itself to refer to the Law (Heb. 9:19; cf. 10:7). Therefore, it is possible that Paul refers to the OT writings with plural τὰ βιβλία.

    To make his request more specific, Paul adds the words μάλιστα τὰς μεμβράνας. μεμβράνα** is a loanword from Latin for the "parchment" used for making books (BAGD). There are two possible significances for Paul's phrase. The first is that it indicates which books, among all those that Paul asks for, he particularly (μάλιστα taken as "most of all, above all, especially") wants. The second possibility is that proposed by Skeat ("Especially the Parchments"), which understands μάλιστα as an equating or defining term so that the phrase is giving a further definition of all the books that Paul wants. On this view μάλιστα would be rendered "that is," and τὰ βιβλία and τὰς μεμβράνας would refer to the same thing. Skeat's documentation of μάλιστα with this meaning (in addition to the more common meaning) elsewhere in Greek literature and in the

PE is convincing, which makes it possible here as well (cf. 1 Tim. 4:10; 5:17; Tit. 1:10[?])."

George W. Knight, *The Pastoral Epistles: A Commentary on the Greek Text*, New International Greek Testament Commentary (Grand Rapids, MI; Carlisle, England: W.B. Eerdmans; Paternoster Press, 1992), 466–467.

6. The city where Paul left his cloak was a major port and, thus, not inconvenient to Timothy: "*Troas* was a seaport on the N.W. coast of Asia Minor, opposite the island of Tenedos, midway between the Hellespont and Cape Lectum, and about ten miles south of the much more ancient Troja (Ilium). The name was an abbreviation of 'Trojan Alexandria.'"James Strahan, "Troas," in *Dictionary of the Apostolic Church (2 Vols.)*, ed. James Hastings (New York: Charles Scribner's Sons, 1916–1918), 620.

8. CHURCH PLANTING STRATEGIES

1. I am fond of the phrase "sovereign surprises," which I first heard from Chaplain (BG) Douglas Lee, US Army Retired. I, thus, want to credit my friend and colleague.
2. Consider J. D. Payne, *Apostolic Church Planting: Birthing New Churches from New Believers* (USA: IVP, 2015).

9. PREPARING THE CHURCH PLANTING PLAN

1. J. I. Packer. *Rediscovering Holiness: Know the Fullness of Life with God* (Grand Rapids, MI: Baker Books, 1992), 69.

APPENDIX 3

1. Charles Haddon Spurgeon, *The Soul Winner: Advice on Effective Evangelism* (New York: Whitaker House, 1995), 123.

APPENDIX 4

1. Martyn Lloyd-Jones, *Studies in the Sermon on the Mount* (Grand Rapids, MI: Eerdmans, 1959), 17.

BIBLIOGRAPHY
A SELECT CHURCH PLANTING BIBLIOGRAPHY

This bibliography is intended as a starting point rather than an exhaustive list. The views presented in these works do not necessarily reflect those of the author; rather, they encompass a range of methods, case studies, and perspectives in the field, with a few exceptions, since 2000 (Leslie Newbiggin's books are an example, which we commend as necessary reading for the church planter). While not offered as a definitive guide to church planting, these peer-reviewed articles, books, and dissertations provide valuable insights into church planting in modern Western societies from diverse theological and regional perspectives. In addition, I have added two bibliography sections that I hope will serve the needs of educators, students, and practitioners. I have created an annotated select bibliography of works concerned with church planting in the Global East and the Global South. Finally, because both Scripture and historical case studies illustrate how the Gospel goes forward to establish new churches through people movement, I have in included a sample bibliography on human migration.

ARTICLES (PRIMARILY CONCERNED WITH CHURCH PLANTING IN THE WEST)

Becker, Paul W., John Carpenter, and Mark Williams. *The New Dynamic Church Planting Handbook*. Faith Mission Publishing, 2003.

Conner, Dustin. "Church Planting Models." Academia, 2012.

Dyck, Thomas M. "Church Planting Strategies." *Canadian Mennonite*, 2006.

Esler, Trevor. "Two Church Planting Paradigms." *International Journal of Frontier Missiology*, 2013.

Garrison, David. "Church Planting Movements." *International Journal of Frontier Missions*, 2004.

Hibbert, Richard Y. "The Place of Church Planting in Mission: Towards a Theological Framework." *Evangelical Review of Theology*, 2009.

Paas, Stefan. "Church Renewal by Church Planting: The Significance of Church Planting for the Future of Christianity in Europe." *Theology Today* 69, no. 4 (2012): 392-401.

Paas, Stefan, and Arjen Vos. "Church Planting and Church Growth in Western Europe: An Analysis." *International Bulletin of Mission Research*, 2016.

Roennfeldt, Peter. *Church Planting*. Adventist UK, 2007.

Snook, Stephen B. "Reaching New People through Church Planting." *Anglican Theological Review*, 2010.

Stetzer, Ed, and Warren Bird. "The State of Church Planting in the United States: Research Overview and Qualitative Study of Primary Church Planting Entities." *Journal of the American Society for Church Growth*, 2008.

Steffen, Thomas A. "Selecting a Church Planting Model That Works." *Missiology* 22, no. 3 (1994): 335-342.

BOOKS (CHURCH PLANTING IN THE WEST)

Allen, Roland. *The Ministry of the Spirit*. Grand Rapids: Eerdmans, 1960.

Allen, Roland. *Missionary Methods: St. Paul's or Ours?* Grand Rapids: Eerdmans, 1962.

Barnes, M. Craig. *The Pastor as Minor Poet: Texts and Subtexts in the Ministerial Life*. Grand Rapids, MI: Eerdmans, 2009.

Becker, Paul W., John Carpenter, and Mark Williams. *The New Dynamic Church Planting Handbook*. Faith Mission Publishing, 2003.

Benesh, Sean. *Metrospiritual: The Geography of Church Planting*. FaithLife Publishers, 2011.

Bolman, Lee G., and Terrence E. Deal. *Reframing Organizations: Artistry, Choice, and Leadership*. San Francisco, CA: Jossey-Bass, 1991.

Bosch, David J. *Transforming Mission: Paradigm Shifts in Theology of Mission*. Maryknoll, NY: Orbis Books, 2011.

Chester, Tim. *Multiplying Churches: Reaching Today's Communities through Church Planting*. Bletchley: Authentic Media, 2006.

Clowney, Edmund P. *The Church: Contours of Christian Theology*. Downers Grove, IL: IVP Academic, 1995.

Dever, Mark. *The Church: The Gospel Made Visible*. Nashville: B&H Publishing Group, 2012.

Dever, Mark. *Nine Marks of a Healthy Church*. Wheaton, IL: Crossway, 2013.

Dyck, Thomas M. *Church Planting Strategies*. Canadian Mennonite, 2006.

Ferguson, Sinclair B. *The Whole Christ: Legalism, Antinomi-*

anism, and Gospel Assurance—Why the Marrow Controversy Still Matters. Wheaton, IL: Crossway, 2016.

Fitch, David E. *Faithful Presence: Seven Disciplines That Shape the Church for Mission*. Downers Grove, IL: InterVarsity Press, 2016.

Glasser, Arthur F., and Charles E. Van Engen. *Announcing the Kingdom: The Story of God's Mission in the Bible*. Grand Rapids, MI: Baker Academic, 2003.

Guder, Darrell L. *Missional Church: A Vision for the Sending of the Church in North America*. Grand Rapids, MI: Eerdmans, 1998.

Helm, David R. *Expositional Preaching: How We Speak God's Word Today*. Wheaton, IL: Crossway, 2014.

Hesselgrave, David J. *Planting Churches Cross-Culturally: North America and Beyond*. 2nd ed. Grand Rapids, MI: Baker Academic, 2000.

Horton, Michael. *The Gospel Commission: Recovering God's Strategy for Making Disciples*. Grand Rapids: Baker Books, 2011.

Hunter, George G. *The Celtic Way of Evangelism: How Christianity Can Reach the West... Again*. Nashville, TN: Abingdon Press, 2000.

Milton, Michael A. *The Secret Life of a Pastor: (And Other Intimate Letters on Ministry)*. Scotland, UK: Christian Focus Publications, 2015.

Milton, Michael A. *A Burden for Revival*. Self-published, 2016.

Murray, Iain H. *The Puritan Hope: Revival and the Interpretation of Prophecy*. Edinburgh: Banner of Truth, 1971.

Murray, Stuart. *Church Planting: Laying Foundations*. Scottdale, PA: Herald Press, 2001.

Newbigin, Lesslie. *The Gospel in a Pluralist Society*. Grand Rapids, MI: Eerdmans, 1989.

Newbigin, Lesslie. *The Household of God: Lectures on the Nature of the Church.* London: SCM Press, 1953.

Newton, Phil A. *The Mentoring Church: How Pastors and Congregations Cultivate Leaders.* Grand Rapids: Kregel Ministry, 2017.

Ott, Craig, and Gene Wilson. *Global Church Planting: Biblical Principles and Best Practices for Multiplication.* Grand Rapids, MI: Baker Academic, 2010.

Paas, Stefan, and Arjen Vos. *Church Planting and Church Growth in Western Europe: An Analysis.* International Bulletin of Mission Research, 2016.

Payne, J.D. *Discovering Church Planting: An Introduction to the Whats, Whys, and Hows of Global Church Planting.* Colorado Springs: Biblica Publishing, 2012.

Payne, J.D. *Apostolic Church Planting: Birthing New Churches from New Believers.* Downers Grove, IL: InterVarsity Press, 2015.

Piper, John. *Let the Nations Be Glad! The Supremacy of God in Missions.* Grand Rapids: Baker Academic, 2003.

Roxburgh, Alan J. *Missional: Joining God in the Neighborhood.* Grand Rapids, MI: Baker Books, 2011.

Snook, Stephen B. *Reaching New People through Church Planting.* Anglican Theological Review, 2010.

Stetzer, Ed, and Warren Bird. *The State of Church Planting in the United States.* Journal of the American Society for Church Growth, 2008.

Stott, John. *The Living Church: Convictions of a Lifelong Pastor.* Downers Grove, IL: IVP Books, 2007.

Van Engen, Charles E. *Mission on the Way: Issues in Mission Theology.* Grand Rapids, MI: Baker Academic, 1996.

Wagner, C. Peter. *Church Planting for a Greater Harvest: A Comprehensive Guide.* Regal Books, 2010.

Whitney, Donald S. *Spiritual Disciplines for the Christian Life.* Colorado Springs, CO: NavPress, 1991.

DISSERTATIONS

Anderson, Randy D. "An Analysis of Attitudes, Values, and Beliefs of Congregants and Leaders of Small Churches Toward Church Planting." PhD diss., The Southern Baptist Theological Seminary, 2009.

Arroyo, Joel. "Discouragement and Supportive Relationships in Latin Pastors Planting Churches in Virginia, North Carolina, and Tennessee." PhD diss., Liberty University, 2023.

Akrong, Joseph G. "An Analysis of the Church Planting Strategies and Methods of the Ghana Baptist Convention and Mission from 1960–2000." PhD diss., Southern Baptist Theological Seminary, 2005.

Barrett, Daniel. "Revitalizing Declining Churches Through Church Planting within the Church of the Nazarene." PhD diss., ProQuest Dissertations Publishing, 2018.

Boyd, Zachary Y. "Experiences in Contemporary Church Planting." PhD diss., ProQuest Dissertations Publishing, 2015.

Crofford, Timothy K. "The Influence of Pastoral Experience on the Success of Church Planters in the Church of the Nazarene and the Wesleyan Church." PhD diss., ProQuest Dissertations Publishing, 2014.

Duncan, Natasha K. "A Correlational Study of Church Planter Emotional Intelligence and Church Sustainability." PhD diss., ProQuest Dissertations Publishing, 2018.

Grant, Luke W. "Theological Analysis of Church Planter Profiles." PhD diss., The Southern Baptist Theological Seminary, 2012.

Hempel, Brian. "Sustainable Church Planting: A Missional Approach." DMin diss., George Fox University, 2015.

Miller, Matthew. "Narratives Church: A Missional Church Planting Path for Cultivating a Unified Theological Vision." PhD diss., Bethel University, 2019.

Priest, Robert J., and Rob DeGeorge. "Doctoral Dissertations on Mission: Ten-Year Update, 2002–2011 (Revised)." *International Bulletin of Missionary Research* 37, no. 4 (2013).

ANNOTATED BIBLIOGRAPHY ON CHURCH PLANTING IN THE GLOBAL SOUTH, GLOBAL EAST, AND MIDDLE EAST

I want to provide additional bibliographic resources for the Global South and Global East (including the Middle East). Some of these sources offer cross-cultural insights, but I think they are helpful in critical thinking about non-Western church planting.

Bevans, Stephen B., and Roger P. Schroeder. *Constants in Context: A Theology of Mission for Today.* Maryknoll, NY: Orbis Books, 2004.

- This comprehensive text includes discussions on contextual theology and mission strategies, especially relevant for church planting in diverse cultural contexts.

Escobar, Samuel. *The New Global Mission: The Gospel from Everywhere to Everyone.* Downers Grove, IL: InterVarsity Press, 2003.

- Escobar, a Latin American missiologist, offers insights into church planting and mission from a Global South perspective, emphasizing the shift of mission leadership to non-Western nations.

Garrison, David. *Church Planting Movements: How God Is Redeeming a Lost World.* Midlothian, VA: WIGTake Resources, 2004.

- Garrison explores effective church planting strategies

and rapid church growth, focusing on movements in South Asia, Southeast Asia, and North Africa.

Hibbert, Richard Yates. "The Place of Church Planting in Mission: Towards a Theological Framework." *Evangelical Review of Theology* 33, no. 4 (2009): 316-331.

○ This article provides a theological framework for church planting in global mission contexts, with implications for regions such as Asia and the Middle East.

Jenkins, Philip. *The Next Christendom: The Coming of Global Christianity*. Oxford: Oxford University Press, 2011.

○ I believe that The Next Christendom is one of the crucial works for the modern global Church. Jenkins examines the shift of Christianity's center to the Global South, discussing church growth and challenges for church planting in Africa, Asia, and Latin America.

Mandryk, Jason. *Operation World: The Definitive Prayer Guide to Every Nation*. 7th ed. Colorado Springs: Biblica Publishing, 2010.

○ Although not exclusively about church planting, this reference provides vital information on the spiritual landscape of every nation, including prayer needs and challenges for planting churches in specific contexts.

Ott, Craig, and Gene Wilson. *Global Church Planting: Biblical Principles and Best Practices for Multiplication*. Grand Rapids, MI: Baker Academic, 2011.

○ Ott and Wilson offer a guide on church planting that addresses the complexities of cross-cultural church growth, with applications particularly suited to non-Western contexts.

Priest, Robert J., and Alvaro L. Nieves. *This Side of Heaven: Race, Ethnicity, and Christian Faith*. Oxford: Oxford University Press, 2007.

○ This book discusses how race and ethnicity affect church

planting and mission work, with practical insights for planting in diverse cultural settings globally.

Samuel, Vinay, and Chris Sugden, eds. *Mission as Transformation: A Theology of the Whole Gospel*. Eugene, OR: Wipf & Stock, 2009.

○ Focusing on the Global South, this volume explores holistic mission strategies and the integration of church planting with social transformation.

Tennent, Timothy C. *Invitation to World Missions: A Trinitarian Missiology for the Twenty-First Century*. Grand Rapids, MI: Kregel Academic, 2010.

ANNOTATED BIBLIOGRAPHY ON HUMAN MIGRATION

The Lord brought about Pentecost through the means of human migration. Jews (to the Jew first and then to the Gentile) dwelling in Jerusalem or had come to dwell there for the sacred Hebrew season. Thus, the Gospel would be proclaimed to representatives of the known world. In one swoop, Jesus brought about a global evangelistic mission. Much is happening in the passage, including reversing the curse at Babel. So, for our purposes, it is crucial to see how God used human migration to reach the world. Thus, I add these volumes as a starter for your research.

Castles, Stephen, Hein de Haas, and Mark J. Miller. *The Age of Migration: International Population Movements in the Modern World*. 6th ed. London: Red Globe Press, 2020.

○ This classic text provides a comprehensive overview of migration trends, drivers, and impacts globally. It's an essential resource for understanding the complexities of migration in both historical and current contexts.

Koser, Khalid. *International Migration: A Very Short Introduction*. Oxford: Oxford University Press, 2007.

○ A concise introduction to migration studies, offering insights into migration's causes, patterns, and consequences. Koser's work is accessible and informative, making it useful for missionaries needing a quick understanding of migration dynamics.

Massey, Douglas S., Joaquín Arango, Graeme Hugo, Ali Kouaouci, Adela Pellegrino, and J. Edward Taylor. *Worlds in Motion: Understanding International Migration at the End of the Millennium*. Oxford: Oxford University Press, 1998.

○ This foundational text presents theories on migration, examining both voluntary and forced movements. It also explores the social and economic effects of migration, which is relevant for church planters interested in the broader impacts of migration on communities.

Portes, Alejandro, and Rubén G. Rumbaut. *Immigrant America: A Portrait*. 4th ed. Berkeley: University of California Press, 2014.

○ This detailed account of immigration to the United States addresses assimilation, identity, and economic impacts, offering insights into the immigrant experience. This is particularly useful for understanding the cultural integration challenges faced by migrant communities.

Sanneh, Lamin. *Whose Religion Is Christianity? The Gospel beyond the West*. Grand Rapids, MI: Eerdmans, 2003.

○ Sanneh explores the shift of Christianity's center to the Global South and how migration has played a role in this transformation. His work is critical for understanding the impact of migration on faith communities and the spread of Christianity.

Stark, Rodney, and Charles Y. Glock. *The New Religious Consciousness*. Berkeley: University of California Press, 1973.

○ Stark's research addresses how migration and social change influence religious adherence and transformations, providing helpful context for how human movement affects religious identity.

Van Hear, Nicholas. *New Diasporas: The Mass Exodus, Dispersal and Regrouping of Migrant Communities*. Seattle: University of Washington Press, 1998.

○ This book examines modern diasporas and their impact on host countries. Van Hear's work provides valuable insights into how migrant communities form and sustain cultural identities, which can inform strategies for engaging diasporic populations.

Vélez-Ibáñez, Carlos G. *Border Visions: Mexican Cultures of the Southwest United States*. Tucson: University of Arizona Press, 1996.

○ Focusing on migration and borderland cultures, this book explores how communities navigate life between cultures. It is particularly relevant for understanding bi-cultural identities and the adaptation processes of migrant groups.

Wimmer, Andreas, and Nina Glick Schiller. *Methodological Nationalism and Beyond: Nation-State Building, Migration and the Social Sciences*. Global Networks, vol. 2, no. 4 (2002): 301–334.

○ This article challenges the assumption that nation-states are the primary units of analysis in migration studies, offering a framework that views migration globally. Useful for understanding transnational connections among migrant groups.

Zolberg, Aristide R. *A Nation by Design: Immigration Policy in the Fashioning of America*. Cambridge, MA: Harvard University Press, 2006.

- This historical account of U.S. immigration policy reveals how states shape and respond to migration. It provides an understanding of how immigration laws influence the movement and settlement of people, which is relevant for church planters working in immigrant-dense areas.

ANNOTATED BIBLIOGRAPHY: EVANGELISM AND MISSIONS IN THE SECULAR AGE

Taylor, Charles. *A Secular Age.* Cambridge, MA: Harvard University Press, 2007.

- Taylor's seminal work explores how Western societies transitioned from a religious to a secular framework. His analysis of "exclusive humanism" and "immanent frames" provides a foundational understanding of secularism's impact on faith, making it essential reading for anyone engaging in evangelism in the secular West.

Milton, Michael A. *From Flanders Fields to the Moviegoer: Philosophical Foundations for a Transcendent Ethical Framework.* Eugene, OR: Wipf and Stock Publications, 2019.

- This book (by the author) examines how Christian ethics and a sense of transcendence can counter secular influences on moral frameworks. I sought to encourage readers to pursue a transcendent, Christ-centered ethic within secular contexts. I pray it is a valuable resource for missionaries and church leaders seeking to engage with our new post-Christian era in the West.

Smith, James K. A. *How (Not) to Be Secular: Reading Charles Taylor.* Grand Rapids, MI: Eerdmans, 2014.

- Smith offers an accessible introduction to Charles Taylor's *A Secular Age,* making complex philosophical ideas more practical and understandable. This book equips readers to interpret Taylor's concepts for everyday ministry, helping Christians live faithfully within secular societies.

Newbigin, Lesslie. *Foolishness to the Greeks: The Gospel and Western Culture.* Grand Rapids, MI: Eerdmans, 1986.

- Newbigin addresses the clash between the Gospel and modern Western secular thought, arguing for a faithful Christian witness that speaks to secularized audiences. His insights are crucial for understanding how the church can maintain its prophetic voice in the West.

McCracken, Brett. *Uncomfortable: The Awkward and Essential Challenge of Christian Community.* Wheaton, IL: Crossway, 2017.

- McCracken's work explores how a robust, countercultural Christian community can stand out in a secularized world. This book encourages a missional approach to church life that engages secular seekers while remaining faithful to biblical truth.

Murray, Paul. *Post-Christendom: Church and Mission in a Strange New World.* Carlisle: Paternoster Press, 2004.

- Murray examines the implications of post-Christendom for Western churches, suggesting new models of mission that respond to secular culture. This work helps us understand how churches can adapt to secular contexts while upholding Christian convictions.

Green, Michael. *Evangelism in the Early Church.* Grand Rapids, MI: Eerdmans, 1970.

- Though historical, Green's work draws parallels between the early church's context and today's secular climate, offering insights into how early Christians engaged diverse, often hostile, audiences. His analysis provides lessons for effective evangelism today.

Davie, Grace. *Religion in Britain: A Persistent Paradox.* 2nd ed. Oxford: Wiley-Blackwell, 2015.

- Davie's exploration of British religiosity reveals the persistence of spirituality within secular societies, challenging assumptions about the decline of faith in the West. Her work is valuable for missionaries understanding secular but spiritually curious societies.

Frost, Michael, and Alan Hirsch. *The Shaping of Things to Come: Innovation and Mission for the 21st-Century Church*. Grand Rapids, MI: Baker Books, 2013.

- This book explores missional models that engage with secularized Western culture, encouraging churches to innovate and reimagine evangelism strategies. Frost and Hirsch provide practical ideas for fostering a missional identity that resonates with the secular world.

Hunter, James Davison. *To Change the World: The Irony, Tragedy, and Possibility of Christianity in the Late Modern World*. Oxford: Oxford University Press, 2010.

- Hunter critiques common Christian approaches to cultural engagement, suggesting a faithful presence within secular culture as an alternative to traditional mission models. His insights are critical for rethinking mission in secular, pluralistic societies.

APPENDICES

1. The Vision and Mission Plan for Kirk O' the Isles
2. Ministry Plan Template
3. First Touch Ministries (a comprehensive plan for parish-based outreach and assimilation
4. The Seven Essential Elements of Visionary-Servant-Leadership
5. An Excursus on Hard Work in the Pastoral Epistles
6. Seven Key Areas for Biblical Assessment in Church Planting
7. The Deep Roots Church Planter Assessment and Pathway
8. Resources for the Deep Roots Church Planting Assessment and Pathway

———

APPENDIX 1
THE VISION AND MISSION PLAN FOR KIRK O' THE ISLES

Note: Our Vision and Mission plan follows the guide offered in *Finding a Vision for Your Church: Assembly Required* by Michael A. Milton (Wipf and Stock, 2024).

MINISTRY PLAN

Kirk of the Isles Presbyterian Church (PCA)

Skidaway Island, Dutch Island, Isle of Hope, Burnside Island, and the Bethesda Area of Savannah

Sponsored by Independent Presbyterian Church and Mission to North America of the Central Georgia Presbytery

Michael A. Milton, Ph.D., Organizing Pastor

Table of Contents

- The Present Situation
- The Target Profile of Skidaway and Southeast Savannah
- The Objective and Possible Obstacles
- The Mother Church

- The Organizing Pastor
- The Story That Begs for a Christ-Centered, Bible-Teaching Church
- First Principles
- Our Vision
- The Name of the Church
- Our Mission
- Our Goals
- Our Strategy
- Philosophy of Ministry
- Ministry Areas (Worship, Education, Fellowship, Church Extension, Mercy Ministry, Christian Schooling, Church Planting)
- Strategic Alliances
- Timetable
- Financial Projection
- Conclusion: Our Greater Vision

The Present Situation

The Session of Independent Presbyterian Church (IPC) has identified Skidaway Island and surrounding areas (Dutch Island, Isle of Hope, Burnside Island) for a new PCA church plant. This desire arose from members residing in these communities who identified a need for a church. After much prayer, the IPC Session committed to targeting this area for a church plant.

This area is ripe for the establishment of a PCA church. The potential reach of this church plant goes beyond individual salvation, presenting an opportunity for a missions resource center for other traditional PCA churches in Savannah and the Central Georgia Presbytery.

The Target Profile of Skidaway and Southeast Savannah

The primary target is Skidaway Island, specifically The

Landings, a community of approximately 8,000 residents. This population mixes professionals and retirees, primarily white and upper-middle income to wealthy. Expanding the target to include surrounding communities raises the total population to around 20,000.

The area hosts several mainline Protestant churches, all leaning towards moderate to liberal theology. The largest congregations are United Methodist, PCUSA, and Southern Baptist churches. The population generally prefers the traditional, mainline worship style, but the need for a biblically faithful Reformed congregation remains unmet.

The Objective and Possible Obstacles

The goal is to establish a PCA church on Skidaway Island that will reach both unchurched individuals and those dissatisfied with current churches. However, obstacles include predictable resistance to the Gospel in North America and resistance from an upper-middle-class community. Additionally, local churches might perceive the new PCA plant as competition, and social networking at The Landings could hinder initial connections.

Strategic prayer will be necessary to overcome these challenges.

The Mother Church

Independent Presbyterian Church (IPC) is a well-established, Christ-centered, Bible-believing congregation known for its evangelism and revitalization efforts. Several session members were enthusiastic about the project, but there may be some detractors within the broader congregation. Despite this, the energy and support from the leadership remain strong.

The Organizing Pastor

As the organizing pastor, I bring experience and alignment with IPC's philosophy of ministry. My previous work planting

Redeemer Presbyterian Church in Overland Park, Kansas, has fostered a strong relationship with IPC. Our shared commitment to biblical, Reformed, liturgical worship and a comprehensive teaching ministry aligns well with the vision for Kirk of the Isles.

After my time in seminary administration and other ministry opportunities, I feel called to return to church planting, and I am eager to begin this work.

The Story That Begs for a Christ-Centered, Bible-Teaching Church

Fred and Denise Jones and their young children moved to Skidaway Island seeking community and spiritual guidance. As they searched for a church home, they were met with teachings that felt distant from the biblical foundations they grew up with. Their dissatisfaction with "tolerance and balance" sermons left them yearning for more profound, Scripture-based teaching. After one exceptionally shallow sermon following a family loss, Denise confided in Fred: "There must be more."

The Burden

This family represents many in Skidaway who are spiritually seeking but feel underserved by existing churches. A Christ-centered, Bible-teaching church could meet the needs of families like the Joneses and bring the light of the Gospel into this community fraught with the spiritual problems arising from postmodern society in an upper-middle income community.

Values, or "First Principles"

Scripture

The Word of God is our ultimate authority. The Bible will inform and guide all aspects of Kirk of the Isles' ministry. We desire for our congregation to grow in the knowledge and grace of Jesus Christ, and this growth comes through a deep engagement with Scripture.

The Great Commission

We are committed to making disciples, baptizing them, and teaching them to observe all Christ commanded (Matthew 28:18-20). This passion for evangelism extends from our families to our community, nation, and the world.

The Reformed Faith

We hold to the doctrines articulated in the Westminster Confession of Faith, believing they faithfully summarize biblical teaching. Our worship will emphasize reverence, simplicity, and expository preaching, and our church will be committed to missions, Christian education, and church planting.

Our Vision

Our vision is for a growing community of changed lives rooted in the Word of God and abounding in grace. We aim to bring the reality of Christ's Lordship to Skidaway Island, Savannah, and beyond through worship, education, and acts of mercy.

The Name of the Church

The name *Kirk of the Isles* reflects our Presbyterian heritage and our geographic focus on Skidaway Island, Isle of Hope, Burnside Island, and Savannah's southern to midtown areas.

Our Mission

Our mission is to gather and grow God's people through the means of grace—Word, Sacrament, and Prayer—so that Christ is worshiped and many come to faith in Him.

Our Goals

1. Establish a vibrant, traditional PCA congregation of 350-500 members.

2. Develop a comprehensive Christian education program, including Pioneer Clubs and youth missions.
3. Initiate a Church Planting Internship program to train future church planters.
4. Plant a new PCA church every four years.

Our Strategy
Philosophy of Ministry

Kirk of the Isles' ministry will be built on four pillars: worship, expository preaching, fellowship, and missions.

- **Worship**: Our services will be characterized by reverence and joy, following a Reformed liturgical format.
- **Preaching**: Sermons will expose and apply the truths of Scripture, working through books of the Bible systematically.
- **Fellowship**: We will create opportunities for families to grow in discipleship and community.
- **Missions**: Our focus on church planting will extend from Skidaway Island to other parts of Savannah and beyond.

Conclusion: Our Greater Vision

We believe God will revive our community soul-by-soul by establishing Kirk of the Isles PCA. We hope that this church, along with those planted from it, will contribute to the renewal of the Church in America.

We pray, as Moses did, "Let Your work appear to Your servants, and Your glory to their children... establish the work of our hands" (Psalm 90:16-17).

APPENDIX 1

APPENDIX 2
A CHURCH PLANTING MINISTRY PLAN TEMPLATE

PART I

Church Name:
Example: Kirk of the Isles Presbyterian Church (PCA)
Target Area:
List specific geographic areas or neighborhoods you aim to serve.
Sponsoring Church or Organization:
Identify the supporting church, denomination, or presbytery.
Organizing Pastor:
Name and background of the organizing pastor.

PART II.

1. Present Situation
- **Community Background**: Describe the spiritual and demographic context of the target area. What is going on here?
- **Need for a New Church**: Explain why the area needs a new church plant. Because of THE BURDEN, I believe the Lord

is calling us to establish a new congregation in TARGET COMMUNITY to VISION (LIFE THE BURDEN).

- **Sponsoring Church's Role**: Outline the mother church's involvement and commitment. Is this relationship clearly defined?

2. Target Profile

- **Demographic Overview**: Summarize the key demographics, such as age, socioeconomic status, and shared religious affiliations. Who are these people? Who are Jack and Susie [COMMUNITY NAME]?

- **Existing Churches**: Describe the types of churches already serving this community and any perceived gaps in their ministry. How is the Gospel going forward? Am I proposing a complimentary work or a competing work? If competing, then how so? Why plant?

- **Unique Needs of the Community**: Identify specific cultural or spiritual needs your church plant aims to meet. Why should we plant this church?

3. Objective and Possible Obstacles

- **Primary Goal**: Define the main objective of the church plant (e.g., reaching the unchurched, serving specific demographics). What is the burden you want to lift from the lives of these people? How will you do so?

- **Anticipated Challenges**: Outline potential obstacles, such as resistance to new churches, demographic barriers, or limited resources.

4. The Story That Inspires the Church Plant

- **Illustrative Story**: Share a short, illustrative story or example of community members who could benefit from the church. The narrative should be based on the information you have discovered in Part II.1-3.

- **Burden for the Lost**: Summarize the church planter's

burden for reaching those disconnected from the current religious landscape.

5. Core Values or First Principles

- **Scripture**: Affirm that the Bible will be the ultimate authority guiding ministry decisions.
- **The Great Commission**: State a commitment to disciple-making, evangelism, and outreach (Matthew 28:18-20).
- **The Reformed Faith**: Describe doctrinal distinctives, such as alignment with the Westminster Confession or other creeds.

6. Vision

- **Vision Statement**: A concise statement describing what you hope the church will become.
- **Geographic and Spiritual Scope**: Detail the intended reach of the church, both geographically and spiritually.

7. Mission

- **Mission Statement**: A clear and brief statement of the church's purpose, focusing on the means of grace (Word, Sacrament, and Prayer) and the goal of worshiping Christ and reaching the lost.

8. Goals

- **Short-term and Long-term Goals**:

1 *Example*: Establish a growing congregation of 200-300 members within five years.

2 Develop Christian education and discipleship programs.

3 Train future leaders and church planters.

4 Plant a new church every 3-5 years.

9. Strategy

- **Worship**: Outline your philosophy and structure for worship, focusing on reverence, joy, and traditional liturgical elements.
- **Preaching**: Describe the preaching style (e.g., expository, systematic through books of the Bible).

- **Fellowship and Community Building**: Detail plans to foster strong community bonds and discipleship opportunities.
- **Missions**: Describe your focus on outreach and church planting both locally and globally.

10. Ministry Areas

- **Worship**: The structure and focus of worship services.
- **Education**: Plans for Sunday School, Bible studies, youth programs, etc.
- **Fellowship**: Describe methods to build community among church members.
- **Church Extension and Mercy Ministries**: Plans for outreach and service projects.
- **Christian Schooling and Church Planting**: If applicable, outline any plans for starting schools or planting new churches.

11. Strategic Alliances

- **Community Partnerships**: List any local organizations or ministries you may partner with.
- **Denominational and Network Support**: Outline any available denominational, presbytery, or other network support.

12. Timetable

- **Phase 1**: Initial community engagement and interest-building (e.g., within the first year).
- **Phase 2**: Begin regular worship services and form initial membership class (years 1-2).
- **Phase 3**: Establish official membership and start local outreach initiatives (years 2-3).
- **Phase 4**: Reach self-sustainability with structured ministries for children, families, and the elderly (year 4+).

13. Financial Projection

- **Startup Costs**: Outline initial funding for facilities, outreach, staff, etc.
- **Operational Budget**: Describe the expected operational expenses and potential sources of revenue.
- **Funding Sources**: List potential sources of support (e.g., sponsoring church, presbytery, donations).

14. Conclusion: A Greater Vision

- **Community Impact**: Summarize how the church plant will impact the community over time.
- **Prayer for God's Blessing**: End with a prayer or scriptural promise, such as Psalm 90:16-17, to invoke God's guidance and favor on the ministry. This prayer could very well become the anchor verse for the work.

APPENDIX 3
FIRST TOUCH MINISTRIES: AN OUTREACH AND ASSIMILATION PLAN FOR THE CHURCH PLANT

"Therefore go and make disciples of all nations, baptizing them in the name of the Father and of the Son and of the Holy Spirit, and teaching them to obey everything I have commanded you. And surely I am with you always, to the very end of the age." (Matthew 28:19-20, NKJV)

The First Touch Ministry
Mobilizing for Ministry Through a Biblical Systems Design for Outreach and Assimilation in the Local Church
Michael A. Milton, Ph.D.

Introduction

Our vision for outreach and ministry requires a systems-based approach, where each ministry and goal integrates seamlessly into the larger mission of the church. This appendix provides an overview of a systems design for effective outreach and assimilation.

Guiding Principles

- **Scriptural Authority, Not Pragmatism**: Our guide is Scripture, not a pragmatic approach that could compromise biblical truth for church growth (2 Timothy 3:16-17).
- **Emphasis on Lay Mobilization**: This approach is as much about equipping lay members for ministry as it is about drawing newcomers into the church.
- **Contextual Adaptability**: This plan arose from a specific setting—an upper-middle-income suburban community in the Midwest—and may need adaptation for other environments.
- **Reformed Theology Compatibility**: A robust outreach strategy aligns with Reformed convictions, affirming that God's sovereignty includes our call to actively share the Gospel (Romans 10:14-15).

I. Biblical Foundations for Outreach and Assimilation

1 The Great Commission compels us to establish an intentional plan for reaching others and integrating them into the church community (Matthew 28:19-20).

2 Biblical Division of Labor directs our approach to outreach (Ephesians 4:11-16). Acts 6 provides a model where the formation of deacons began with a specific need, leading to a structured order and a subsequent revival (Acts 6:1-7).

3 The Priesthood of All Believers encourages each member to participate in ministry, empowering the church to "melt down the saints" for the work of the Kingdom, as Cromwell put it in the English Civil War—employing all resources for advancing God's mission (1 Peter 2:4-5, 9-10).

4 The Example of the Early Church shows that mobilizing a broad base of church members is essential (Acts 8:4; Colossians 4:10-17).

II. Goals of First Touch Ministries

1 Submission to God's Plan: To surrender our lives and ministry to God's design for His church (Proverbs 19:21).

2 Equipping Pastors: To develop pastors who serve by equipping the saints through teaching and example (Ephesians 4:11-12).

3 Every-Member Ministry: To create a culture where each member is engaged in ministry, contributing to the building up of Christ's body (1 Corinthians 12:12-27).

4 Kingdom Growth: To focus on growing Christ's Kingdom, ultimately becoming a New Testament church "on the move" for the Kingdom of Christ (Acts 2:42-47).

III. System Design Overview

God works systematically (Ephesians 1:11), and we reflect His order in our approach to ministry. The mission of our church—"to Gather, Grow, and Send forth strong disciples of Jesus Christ"—is pursued through a structured system:

1 Pre-Evangelism and Outreach: Preparing the church community for intentional, relationship-driven outreach.

2 Evangelism and Assimilation: Providing clear pathways for newcomers to connect and integrate into the church.

3 Discipleship and Lay Mobilization: Empowering members for service and ministry within the church and beyond.

IV. The Plan for Outreach and Assimilation

I. Pre-Evangelism and Outreach

Annual Leadership Planning Retreat

- Plan ministry events and reinforce vision and goals.

Annual Great Commission Lay Training

- **Year One**: Training in evangelism through role-playing and real-life applications.
- **Year Two**: Introduction to apologetics, equipping members to address common objections to faith.
- **Year Three**: Tailored training based on community needs.

Annual Cycle for Outreach Events

Outreach aligns with the church's annual rhythm:

- **September**: Community events as natural points of entry.
- **Advent/Christmas**: Special worship services.
- **Easter**: Resurrection celebration services.
- **July**: Summer events like Vacation Bible School.

Event Advertising

Outreach and advertising efforts display the church's warmth and love, drawing others in with "the beauty of the Body of Christ."

II. Evangelism and Assimilation

First Touch Ministry

The heart of this outreach system, *First Touch*, aims to make a meaningful connection with every visitor:

- **Touchpoints**: From parking lot greeters to ushers and intentional follow-up, each interaction serves as a gentle welcome into the life of the church.

Assimilation Process

1 First Visit: Welcoming greeters, ushers, and intentional follow-up after worship.

2 Second Visit: Personal follow-up and invitation to the Pastor's Welcome Class.

3 Pastor's Welcome Class: An introduction to the church's faith and practices, creating an inclusive environment where visitors can connect with church leaders and fellow members.

III. Discipleship and Lay Mobilization

Regular Care and Assimilation

- **Flock Care**: Ongoing care through small groups and regular elder and deacon visits.
- **Discover Class**: A yearly course to help members discern their gifts and interests for ministry, allowing each to find their place in the body of Christ.

V. Necessary Components for Success

1 Leadership Involvement and Engagement: Personal meetings with leaders to assess and refine the system.

2 Congregational Communication: Letters from the pastor, congregational meetings, and recruitment efforts.

3 Evaluation and Adaptation: Regular assessments, with adjustments discussed at annual ministry retreats.

4 Testimony Service: A dedicated service to celebrate new believers and transformed lives, reflecting God's work in the church (Acts 6:7).

This outreach plan, *First Touch Ministries*, is designed to foster a church environment where the lost are reached, believers are equipped, and Christ's kingdom grows, all under the guiding authority of Scripture and in harmony with Reformed principles.

> *"When we, in our churches, forget our purpose to be the fragrance of Christ in a world that needs Him, we drift from the reason for our existence. We are called not to build kingdoms, but to proclaim the Kingdom, trusting God with the growth."* —Charles Haddon Spurgeon[1]

APPENDIX 4
THE SEVEN ESSENTIAL ELEMENTS OF VISIONARY-SERVANT-LEADERSHIP

"I am the good shepherd. The good shepherd gives His life for the sheep" (John 10:11 NKJV).

Leadership: An Instrument of Divine Calling

Leadership is not a self-initiated endeavor but a response to God's initiating call. When we make leadership our primary focus, we risk creating a human-centered program that misses the mark of divine mission. I recall an elder council member saying, *"Give the dogs what the dogs want to eat,"* suggesting that church leadership should cater to public demand. But I reminded him that we are not feeding "dogs" but shepherding God's flock, which is undertaken under His authority (1 Peter 5:2-3). Too often, a self-centered approach to leadership can lead to a culture that is narcissistic and ultimately harmful.

Authentic, biblical leadership is not about satisfying desires but answering God's call. Leadership begins with God's burden and vision, where He is the subject, and we, as human leaders, are the recipients and channels of His direction. While God alone holds ultimate glory, He calls human leaders to steward His vision, just as He called Moses, David, and other shepherd-leaders of Israel (Exodus 3:10; 1 Samuel 16:12-13). In the ministry of reconciliation entrusted to us (2 Corinthians 5:18-19), our leadership is to mirror Christ's humility and service, guided by God's burden, vision, and values.

Introduction

Christian leadership is founded upon the life and teachings of Jesus Christ and the apostolic witness. In Matthew's Gospel, Jesus rebukes worldly models of power: *"You know that the rulers of the Gentiles lord it over them, and their great ones exercise authority over them. Yet it shall not be so among you"* (Matthew 20:25-26 NKJV). Likewise, Peter offers counsel to leaders, saying, *"Shepherd the flock of God which is among you, serving as overseers, not by compulsion but willingly, not for dishonest gain but eagerly; nor as being lords over those entrusted to you, but being examples to the flock"* (1 Peter 5:2-3 NKJV). Against this scriptural foundation, Moses is a biblical example of visionary leadership, guided by the redemptive narrative themes of Creation, Fall, Redemption, and Restoration.

The Seven Essential Elements of Visionary-Servant Leadership

1 The Visionary-Servant Leader of God Identifies the Vision

True vision is born from a divine burden—God's call to address a particular need within His creation. Abraham Kuyper teaches that God's sovereignty extends to all spheres of life, meaning that our burdened calling may encompass not only individuals but families, communities, and even nations. For the church planter or pastor, the vision emerges from a burden aligned with God's heart, just as Moses heard God say, *"I have surely seen the oppression of My people"* (Exodus 3:7 NKJV).

- **Transactional Failure**: Vision driven solely by quantifiable goals, neglecting the spiritual core.
- **Visionary-Servant Response**: Rooting the vision in God's burden and pursuing His redemptive purpose.

2 The Visionary-Servant Leader of God Embodies the Vision

Embodying the vision requires that the leader internalize and live out the mission daily, becoming a visible witness of the calling. Moses lived this through his perseverance with Israel, enduring trials as he led them (Exodus 14:13-14).

- **Transactional Failure**: Performing leadership duties without a heart of commitment to the vision.
- **Visionary-Servant Response**: Living a life consistent with God's redemptive plan, exemplified in personal conduct.

3 The Visionary-Servant Leader of God Equips Others to Execute the Vision

Effective leadership means equipping others to take part in the vision, as Jesus empowered His disciples to perform greater works (John 14:12). Moses equipped Israel by giving them the law, guiding them in obedience to God's commands (Exodus 20).

- **Transactional Failure**: Providing resources without fostering spiritual depth.
- **Visionary-Servant Response**: Equipping others with tools and training, grounded in spiritual maturity.

4 The Visionary-Servant Leader of God Encourages Others to Embrace the Vision

Visionary leaders inspire others to adopt the vision by creating a culture of genuine love and commitment to God's purposes. Moses consistently encouraged Israel, interceding for them and reminding them of God's faithfulness (Deuteronomy 31:6).

- **Transactional Failure**: Motivating with rewards or recognition rather than divine purpose.
- **Visionary-Servant Response**: Fostering a deep-seated love for God's redemptive vision through relational discipleship.

5 The Visionary-Servant Leader of God Endows the Vision

To endow a vision means not only to provide financial resources but also to secure spiritual support. Moses sought God's promises as an endowment for his mission to lead Israel to freedom (Exodus 3:8).

- **Transactional Failure**: Emphasizing material endowments while neglecting spiritual ones.
- **Visionary-Servant Response**: Ensuring that the vision is sustained by both prayerful and practical support.

6 The Visionary-Servant Leader of God Enfolds Others into the Ecosystem of the Vision

True leaders invite others to become integral to the life cycle of the vision. Jesus exemplified this through the Great Commission, commanding His followers to make disciples (Matthew 28:19-20). Moses established a covenantal community, grounded in God's law (Numbers 1).

- **Transactional Failure**: Treating inclusion as a statistic rather than a covenantal commitment.
- **Visionary-Servant Response**: Building a covenant community where each person's role is essential to the mission.

7 The Visionary-Servant Leader of God Evaluates the Evolution of the Vision

Ongoing assessment is crucial to leadership, as seen in Moses preparing Israel and Joshua for the Promised Land (Deuteronomy 31:7-8). This reflective evaluation ensures alignment with God's redemptive work.

- **Transactional Failure**: Focusing on metrics alone without regard for spiritual growth.
- **Visionary-Servant Response**: Regularly evaluating the mission's spiritual and practical alignment with God's overarching redemptive plan.

Summary

The essence of visionary servant-leadership lies in following Christ's example and operating within the scriptural narrative of Creation, Fall, Redemption, and Restoration. This approach contrasts with transactional leadership, focusing instead on lifting burdens and realizing divine visions through a biblically grounded mission.

Christian leadership begins with a relationship with Jesus Christ, the ultimate pattern for self-giving service and faithful burden-bearing. When we align ourselves with God's sovereignty and grace, we unlock the potential to lead in a way that reflects His heart for His people.

"I know of nothing that I would more desire for myself than to be truly humble and to be truly filled with the Holy Spirit." — Martyn Lloyd-Jones, *Studies in the Sermon on the Mount*[1]

APPENDIX 5
AN EXCURSUS FROM THE PASTORAL EPISTLES ON THE CHURCH PLANTER AND HARD WORK

"Wage the good warfare" (1 Timothy 1:18 ESV).

Hard Work in the Pastoral Epistles

Contrary to what may be portrayed in literature or popular media, the biblical vision of pastoral ministry demands diligence and hard work. The term "shepherd," as used for ministers, echoes the toil and humility required of a shepherd's daily duties. Our Lord Jesus draws on this Old Testament imagery, applying the shepherding motif to the work of the Christian minister in all aspects of this sacred office. Shepherding is labor-intensive, often messy, and typically far removed from the esteem of polite society. In ancient times, shepherds were not likely to be honored guests at a burgher's banquet, yet the shepherd metaphor is one God chose to embody the essence of pastoral ministry.

Like the shepherd, the church planter must care deeply for the flock—though the flock is not his own. The shepherd knows that the flock belongs to the Master, to whom he will one day give account (Hebrews 13:17). He relates to the flock as a father to his beloved children, guiding them away from harm and leading them to green pastures of health and vitality (Psalm 23:2-4). His role encompasses tending to wounds, correcting strays, guarding against external threats, and knowing the flock intimately, including their individual needs and dangers. The good shepherd is also a keen student, observing the terrain, recognizing predators, identifying sustenance, and anticipating seasonal shifts (John 10:3-4). In this work, he may rely on fellow elders and deacons to support and provide accountability, but his role remains unique—he is the one called to bring the flock safely home to the Master.

While the shepherd's work is spiritually rewarding, it also involves countless sacrifices. His wages are often modest compared to his labor, though there may be moments of quiet reward: a crisp autumn night under the stars, the peaceful sounds of contented sheep, the birth of a lamb, or the silent gratitude of a ewe during lambing season. In all these, he finds purpose and fulfillment, yet he must also accept the lowliness, isolation, and spiritual challenges of the role.

"Counting the Cost"

For those considering the calling of church planting—a role in which ministers are set apart as evangelists to gather and nurture new communities in Christ—it is imperative to count the cost before embarking. Our Lord's words provide a solemn reminder:

> "Whoever does not bear his own cross and come after me cannot be my disciple. For which of you, desiring to build a tower, does not first sit down and count the cost, whether he has enough to complete it? ... So

therefore, any one of you who does not renounce all that he has cannot be my disciple" (Luke 14:27-33 ESV).

In the spirit of this calling, I present several examples from the Pastoral Epistles that illustrate the commitment and "hard work" involved in church planting. By "hard work," we mean "actively engaged in ministry," not passive. This is not the work of a scholar in the study but the pastoral-scholar in the field of spiritual opposition. Paul's instructions to Timothy reveal a range of expectations that can serve as a blueprint for ministry, illustrating the profound dedication needed in this work. I encourage readers to study each example in context, explore the original Greek where possible, and reflect on how these actions resonate with your own ministry.

HARD WORK IN THE PASTORAL EPISTLES

- **Wage the Good Warfare**: "This charge I entrust to you, Timothy, my child… that by them you may wage the good warfare" (1 Timothy 1:18).
- **Train Yourself**: "Train yourself for godliness" (1 Timothy 4:7).
- **Command and Teach**: "Command and teach these things" (1 Timothy 4:11).
- **Set an Example**: "Set the believers an example in speech, in conduct" (1 Timothy 4:12).
- **Devote, Do Not Neglect, Practice, Immerse, Persist**: "Devote yourself to the public reading of Scripture, to exhortation, to teaching. Do not neglect the gift… Practice these things, immerse yourself in them, so that all may see your progress. Keep a close watch on yourself and on the teaching.

Persist in this, for by so doing you will save both yourself and your hearers" (1 Timothy 4:13-16).
- **Govern, Preach, Teach**: "Let the elders who rule well be considered worthy of double honor, especially those who labor in preaching and teaching" (1 Timothy 5:17-18).
  - Rule or Govern (προΐστημι *proistēmi*): to lead or manage.
  - Preaching (λόγος *logos*): message or proclamation.
  - Teaching (διδασκαλία *didaskalia*): doctrine or instruction.
- **Teach and Urge**: "Teach and urge these things" (1 Timothy 6:2).
- **Fight the Good Fight, Take Hold**: "Fight the good fight of the faith. Take hold of the eternal life to which you were called" (1 Timothy 6:12).
- **Strive Like a Soldier and an Athlete**: "No soldier gets entangled in civilian pursuits... An athlete is not crowned unless he competes according to the rules. It is the hard-working farmer who ought to have the first share of the crops" (2 Timothy 2:4-6).
- **Preach, Do the Work of an Evangelist, and Fulfill Your Ministry**: "Preach the word; be ready in season and out of season; reprove, rebuke, and exhort, with complete patience and teaching... As for you, always be sober-minded, endure suffering, do the work of an evangelist, fulfill your ministry" (2 Timothy 4:1-5).
- **Travel When Necessary**: "Do your best to come to me soon" (2 Timothy 4:9).
- **Put Things in Order**: "This is why I left you in Crete, so that you might put what remained into

order, and appoint elders in every town as I directed you" (Titus 1:5).
- **Declare, Exhort, Rebuke**: "Declare these things; exhort and rebuke with all authority.
  - Speak (λαλέω *laleō*): to talk or proclaim.
- **Remind**: "Remind them to be submissive to rulers and authorities, to be obedient… to show perfect courtesy toward all people" (Titus 3:1-2). Let no one disregard you" (Titus 2:15).

Reflections for Further Study

As you examine each of these exhortations, consider how the action verbs in these passages translate into real-life applications for ministry. Reflect on the weight of these responsibilities and ask yourself: How might you embody these actions as a church planter or pastor? Are you prepared to devote yourself fully to the charge entrusted to you? For as Paul's words make clear, church planting is not for the fainthearted but for those willing to labor steadfastly for the glory of God and the good of His people.

Here are six reflection and discussion questions designed to encourage thoughtful engagement with each key aspect of hard work in church planting, especially as outlined in the excursus on "hard work" from the Pastoral Epistles:

1 Waging the Good Warfare

- Paul charges Timothy to "wage the good warfare" (1 Timothy 1:18). Reflect on what it means to "wage" spiritual warfare as a church planter. How do you practically engage in spiritual battles within your ministry context? In what ways can you prepare yourself and your congregation to face spiritual opposition?

2 Training for Godliness

- "Train yourself for godliness" (1 Timothy 4:7). Godliness here is not merely ethical living but involves a deep commitment to spiritual disciplines. What practical steps are you taking to train yourself in godliness? How does this personal training impact your ability to lead others in discipleship and spiritual growth?

3 Setting an Example in Conduct and Speech

- Paul urges Timothy to "set the believers an example in speech, in conduct" (1 Timothy 4:12). In what areas of your own life do you feel challenged to be an example to others? How might your speech and conduct serve as a model of Christ-like character for new believers in your church plant?

4 Devotion, Persistence, and Guarding Sound Doctrine

- "Devote yourself to the public reading of Scripture, to exhortation, to teaching" (1 Timothy 4:13-16). This passage speaks to a ministry of perseverance and constant watchfulness. How are you ensuring that you stay devoted to the core practices of reading, teaching, and applying Scripture? In what ways are you guarding sound doctrine while fostering growth in your congregation?

5 Engaging in Evangelistic Work with Patience and Teaching

- Paul instructs, "Do the work of an evangelist, fulfill your ministry" (2 Timothy 4:5). How are you balancing the need for evangelism with the patience required for teaching? Reflect on how you can practice both patience and boldness as you share the Gospel in your church plant, especially with those who may be resistant or slow to embrace the faith.

6 Ordering and Structuring Ministry for Effective Growth

- "Put what remained into order, and appoint elders in every town" (Titus 1:5). Church planting involves more than gathering people; it also requires establishing a sustainable structure. How do you envision ordering and structuring your ministry to enable long-term growth and accountability? How do you balance the urgency of evangelism with the patience required to raise and appoint faithful leaders?

APPENDIX 6
SEVEN KEY AREAS FOR BIBLICAL ASSESSMENT IN CHURCH PLANTING

"But seek first the kingdom of God and His righteousness, and all these things shall be added to you" (Matthew 6:33 NKJV).

---

1. Personal Sense of Call

A foundational element in assessing a church planter is their personal sense of divine calling. Biblical accounts illustrate how God's call often comes with a deep, personal conviction. Jeremiah speaks of a "fire shut up in [his] bones" that he cannot contain (Jeremiah 20:9), while Paul describes being "compelled" to preach, saying, "Woe to me if I do not preach" (1 Corinthians 9:16).

A church planter should demonstrate a profound, God-given sense of calling that transcends career ambition. Key questions to consider include:

- **Divine Compulsion:** Does the church planter feel a divine compulsion toward this work? How is this burden articulated and demonstrated in their life?

- **Confirming Moments**: Can they identify specific experiences that confirmed their calling? Was there a turning point leading to the call to plant a church in this place?
- **Spiritual Burden**: Is there a holy restlessness for those they seek to reach, revealing that this burden comes from Scripture? (If married) Is this burden shared by their family?

2. Affirmation by the Body of Christ

Scripture shows that a calling is often confirmed through the Body of Christ. In Acts 13:2-3, the Holy Spirit calls Paul and Barnabas, with the church in Antioch affirming this call by laying hands on them and sending them off.

Assessment should involve input from mature believers who have witnessed the church planter's ministry over time. Consider:

- **Community Endorsement**: Do mature Christians see God's calling and gifting evident in the church planter's life?
- **Formal Recognition**: Have church leaders laid hands on this individual, publicly affirming their calling?
- **Fruitfulness**: Is there observable fruit from previous ministry work that affirms their readiness?

3. Ability to Articulate a Call to a Specific Place

Church planting often involves a call to a specific community or demographic, much as Paul was called to minister among the Gentiles (Acts 9:15; Galatians 2:7-8). A church planter must clearly articulate why they feel called to a specific area.

Key questions include:

- **Place-Specific Calling**: Can the church planter explain why they feel called to this community?
- **Understanding of Community Needs**: Are they knowledgeable about the unique cultural and spiritual needs of this area?
- **Demonstrated Commitment**: Have they undertaken

research or ministry efforts to understand and engage with the community?

4. Demonstrated Resilience and Endurance

Resilience is crucial for church planters, who may encounter opposition, loneliness, and spiritual warfare. Paul frequently wrote of his trials, from imprisonment to hardships, yet continued to serve by relying on God's grace (2 Corinthians 11:23-28).

When assessing resilience, consider:

- **Past Trials:** Has the church planter faced ministry trials that reveal their ability to endure?
- **Spiritual Foundation:** Do they show strong grounding in prayer, Scripture, and reliance on the Holy Spirit?
- **Preparation for Adversity:** Are they mentally and spiritually prepared to face isolation, discouragement, and potential adversity in church planting?

5. A Shepherd's Heart for the Flock

A church planter must love people, reflecting Christ's own heart for His flock. Jesus describes Himself as the "good shepherd" who "lays down his life for the sheep" (John 10:11). A church planter should demonstrate sacrificial love for others.

In assessing this quality, consider:

- **Compassion for Others:** Does the church planter exhibit genuine compassion and care for those they are called to serve?
- **Humility and Kindness:** Do they approach people with humility and a readiness to listen and understand?
- **Commitment to Discipleship:** Are they dedicated to nurturing, discipling, and guiding their future congregation toward maturity in Christ?

6. Demonstrated Faithfulness in Sharing the Gospel of Jesus Christ

Faithfulness in sharing the Gospel is fundamental to church planting, requiring the planter to effectively communicate Christ's message both publicly and privately. The Apostle Paul modeled this by boldly proclaiming the Gospel in public and encouraging believers one-on-one (Acts 20:20).

Key questions for this area include:

- **Public Proclamation**: Does the church planter demonstrate effectiveness in public preaching, presenting the Gospel clearly and confidently?
- **Private Teaching and Counseling**: Are they equally effective in sharing the Gospel privately, through teaching, counseling, or personal conversations?
- **Consistent Witness**: Is there evidence that they regularly engage in Gospel conversations, both with believers and nonbelievers?

7. Demonstrated Nature, Gifts, and Practice of Exercising Visionary-Servant Leadership

The church planter must not only possess a personal vision for ministry but also the ability to lead and inspire others in a Christ-centered, servant-oriented way. Jesus' leadership exemplifies this in John 10:11, "I am the good shepherd. The good shepherd gives His life for the sheep" (John 10:11 NKJV).

As outlined in Appendix 4, biblical leadership involves embodying the vision God has given, equipping others, and serving humbly. This includes building up ministry teams, exercising authority with humility, and constantly aligning oneself with God's call (see 1 Peter 5:2-3; Matthew 20:25-28). Key aspects of this quality include:

- **Vision Alignment**: Does the church planter possess a God-centered vision that guides their ministry direction?
- **Team Development**: Do they effectively equip and empower others to take part in the mission, as seen in Christ's leadership with His disciples?
- **Servant-Hearted Authority**: Do they exercise authority

in a way that mirrors Christ's humble service and reflects genuine care for those they lead?

Summary

These seven biblical principles establish a comprehensive framework for evaluating a church planter's readiness for ministry. Grounded in Scripture and the Spirit's leading, they provide a well-rounded lens through which the Body of Christ can discern God's calling and support the church planter in their mission. Through these key areas, we seek to uphold the holy call of church planting as a work of obedience to Christ's Great Commission, conducted by those who lead not in their own strength but in submission to the Spirit.

APPENDIX 7
THE DEEP ROOTS CHURCH PLANTER ASSESSMENT AND PATHWAY

The Lord of the Church alone assesses, calls, and equips those who will go in His name to further the kingdom of God. Yet, the Bible shows that God accomplishes His will ordinarily through His people in a covenanted community. Our proposed assessment is a Biblical-theological framework that seeks to validate the "Seven Key Areas for Biblical Assessment in Church Planting" (Appendix 6) in the life and ministry of the church planting candidate through confidential reflections by friends or family and past supervisors or colleagues in ministry. Added is the candidate's self-disclosure through a testimony narrative and self-assessment. These are conducted in an online confidential survey on one of the trusted survey platforms (e.g., Typeform, Zoho). The Assessment Team prepares for the candidate through prayerful reading and considering the confidential responses. An interview follows. After a discussion, prayer, and consideration, the Team counsels the candidate (not a "decision," which we believe should be made locally).

Below is a pathway diagram and outline for the church

planter assessment process, starting from local church prayer and going to the next steps after assessment. This pathway guides candidates, assessors, and church leadership through a structured, prayerful, and biblically grounded evaluation.

KEY POINTS TO REMEMBER:

The guiding principles that undergird the Deep Roots Assessment include:

- **Prayerful Foundation**: Each step is undergirded by prayer, seeking the Holy Spirit's guidance.
- **Biblical Grounding**: The Seven Key Areas for Biblical Assessment serve as the framework, ensuring alignment with scriptural qualifications.
- **Confidentiality**: All personal and reference materials are handled with privacy and respect.
- **Community Involvement**: The process involves input from various members of the Body of Christ, reflecting the communal nature of discernment.
- **Supportive Approach**: The goal is to affirm and support the candidate's calling, providing guidance and resources for growth.
- **Counsel, not Decision**: The Deep Roots assessment provides biblical, prayerful, comprehensive consideration that leads to counsel for the candidate and the respective church or ministry.

CHURCH PLANTER ASSESSMENT PATHWAY

1 Local Church Prayer and Discernment

- **Description**: The process begins with the local church praying and seeking God's guidance for church planting opportunities and potential candidates within the congregation.

- **Action Steps**:
    - Church leadership encourages the congregation to pray for new ministry initiatives.
    - Identification of individuals who may be sensing a call to church planting.
    - Elders and pastors remain attentive to members exhibiting gifts and calling.

2 Candidate Initiates Contact

Description: An individual feeling called to church planting expresses interest in church leadership.

- **Action Steps**:
    - The candidate meets with a pastor or elder to discuss their sense of calling.
    - Initial discussions about the candidate's experiences, spiritual gifts, and desire for ministry.
    - Church leadership guides the discernment process.

3 Judicatory Response and Initial Approval

Description: The appropriate church judicatory (e.g., denominational board, presbytery) is notified of the candidate's interest.

- **Action Steps:**
  - Church leadership contacts the judicatory to inform them of the potential candidate.
  - The judicatory provides initial guidelines and requirements for assessment.
  - Formal approval is granted to proceed with the assessment process.

4 Assessment Preparation

Description: The candidate completes preparatory materials to aid in the assessment.

- **Action Steps:**
  - **Candidate Completes the Following**:
    - **Personal Testimony**: A three-page narrative of God's work in their life.
    - **Personal Patterns and Preferences Self-Review**:
      - Life narrative identifying strengths, struggles, and post-conversion focus areas.
      - Questionnaire responding to the Seven Key Areas for Biblical Assessment in Church Planting (Appendix 6).
  - **References Complete Questionnaires**:
    - Two personal references (family or friends) respond to questions related to the Seven Key Areas.
    - Two former ministry supervisors provide assessments based on their experiences with the candidate.
      - **Submission:**

- All materials are submitted confidentially online (e.g., Typeform, Zoho).

5 Assessment Team Review

Description: The assessment team reviews all preparatory materials before the meeting.

- **Action Steps**:
  - Each assessor reads and reflects on the candidate's submissions and reference feedback.
  - Assessors note areas of strength and areas needing further exploration.
  - Preparation of questions and topics for the upcoming interview.

6 Prayerful and Confidential Discussion

Description: The assessment team meets to discuss findings and prepare for the interview.

- **Action Steps**:
  - The team gathers for collective prayer, seeking the Holy Spirit's guidance.
  - Confidential discussion of the candidate's materials, focusing on the Seven Key Areas.
  - Alignment of assessment objectives and interview strategy.

7 Assessment Interview

Description: The candidate participates in a formal interview with the assessment team.

- **Action Steps**:
    - Scheduling of the interview at a mutually agreeable time.
    - Conducting the interview, addressing the Seven Key Areas:

1 Personal Sense of Call
2 Affirmation by the Body of Christ
3 Ability to Articulate a Call to a Specific Place
4 Demonstrated Resilience and Endurance
5 A Shepherd's Heart for the Flock
6 Faithfulness in Sharing the Gospel
7 Visionary-Servant Leadership Abilities

- Providing the candidate the opportunity to ask questions and share further insights.

8 Deliberation and Prayer

Description: After the interview, the assessment team deliberates on reaching a consensus.

- **Action Steps**:
    - Team members share observations and impressions from the interview.
    - Prayerful consideration of the candidate's readiness and suitability.
    - Compilation of collective feedback and recommendations.

9 Providing Counsel to the Candidate

Description: The assessment team communicates their findings to the candidate.

- **Action Steps**:
    - Preparation of a written summary of the assessment results.
    - Meeting with the candidate to discuss the outcome.
    - Recommendations may include:

1. **Further Reflection Needed**: Identifying specific areas for growth before proceeding.
2. **Affirmation with Suggestions**: Recognizing readiness with recommendations for continued development.
3. **Full Affirmation ("Go")**: Endorsing the candidate's preparedness to proceed without reservations.

10 Formal Communication to Judicatory

Description: The assessment team's conclusions are communicated to the appropriate church authorities.

- **Action Steps**:
    - Submission of the assessment report to the candidate's respective judicatory.
    - Providing necessary documentation and recommendations for the candidate's next steps.
    - Coordination with the judicatory on any required approvals or support.

11 Next Steps and Ongoing Support

Description: Based on the assessment, the candidate and church leadership plan subsequent actions.

- **Action Steps:**
    - If affirmed, the candidate begins formal preparations for church planting (e.g., training, fundraising, establishing support networks).
    - If further development is recommended, the candidate engages in specified growth opportunities (e.g., mentorship, additional ministry experience, theological education).
    - Ongoing prayer and support from the local church and assessment team.
    - Regular check-ins to monitor progress and encourage.
    - If desired, the sponsoring pastor (presumably the supervising pastor of the candidate) of the local church or next-level judicatory may request the Assessment Team to reconvene and receive a further evaluation based on the "Seven Key Areas for Biblical Assessment in Church Planting" (Appendix 6). The Team will meet in prayer and discussion and provide another response using the same criterea.

PATHWAY OUTLINE

1. Local Church Prayer and Discernment
↓
2. Candidate Initiates Contact

↓

3. Judicatory Response and Initial Approval
↓
4. Assessment Preparation
- Candidate completes testimony and self-review
- References complete questionnaires

↓ The assessment Team assumes the custody of the confidential responses.

5. Assessment Team Review
↓
6. Prayerful and Confidential Discussion
↓
7. Assessment Interview
↓
8. Deliberation and Prayer
↓
9. Providing Counsel to the Candidate
↓
10. Formal Communication to Judicatory
↓
11. Next Steps and Ongoing Support

This pathway provides a structured approach that ensures each step is grounded in prayer, biblical principles, and thorough evaluation. It emphasizes the importance of community discernment, personal reflection, and alignment with God's calling.

You can use this outline to create a diagram using flowchart software or presentation tools (e.g., Canva) to represent each step and the flow between them visually. Figure 1 shows a simplified version. The QR code will take you to a website version of the Assessment Pathway.

APPENDIX 7

Figure 1: Deep Roots Church Planting Assessment Pathway. © Michael A. Milton. It may be used when purchasing this book for education.

QR Code for Figure 1 as a website.

APPENDIX 8
RESOURCES FOR THE DEEP ROOTS CHURCH PLANTING ASSESSMENT AND PATHWAY

The following items are suggested for use in the assessment process.

INTRODUCTION FOR ASSESSORS

Dear Assessors,

Thank you for participating in this sacred task of assessing the readiness and suitability of a prospective church planter. Your role is vital, as you represent the discernment and guidance of Christ's Body, helping ensure that those who embark on this challenging mission are well-prepared and firmly rooted in their calling.

This assessment is not a mere checklist of skills or qualifications. Rather, it is a process grounded in prayer, Scripture, and Spirit-led discernment. The goal is not to evaluate this individual as if they were a candidate for secular employment, nor to measure them against worldly standards of success or leadership potential. As we gather for this purpose, it is essential to remember that assessing church planters is not about talent management, filling a role, or hiring a branch leader; it is an intentional, biblically-based inquiry into the evidence of God's calling, the presence of spiritual gifts, and the signs of godly character.

This guide highlights seven key areas that reflect biblical and pastoral integrity, resilience, and vision. As you prayerfully consider each element, allow the Holy Spirit to guide your observations, insights, and questions. Remember that you collectively steward God's mission by affirming those He has called, equipped, and prepared for this vital work.

We also recognize the value of your unique perspectives—lay leaders, pastors, experienced planters, and senior ministers alike. Your contributions, grounded in your knowledge of Scripture and personal experience, bring invaluable depth to this process. Additionally, the insights of wives and other mature women of the church may provide an essential perspective on aspects of family life, relational qualities, and a holistic view of readiness for ministry.

May the Lord grant you discernment, compassion, and wisdom as you fulfill this calling to assess in accordance with His Word. May your efforts serve as a blessing to this candidate and as a safeguard for the congregation, they may one day serve.

In Christ's service,

[Designated Team Leader]

COMPOSITION AND PURPOSE OF THE ASSESSMENT TEAM

The assessment team for a church planter candidate is intentionally diverse, drawing from lay leaders, experienced pastors, seasoned church planters, senior ministers, and, when appropriate, the wives of the candidate and of assessors. This varied composition enriches the evaluation process by bringing perspectives from those who have served in different capacities within the church. The team's purpose is to discern, through prayerful examination and discussion, whether the candidate is spiritually and practically prepared for the unique calling of church planting. Each member contributes insights rooted in Scripture, pastoral experience, and spiritual wisdom, assessing the candidate's alignment with the biblical standards for ministry and the specific challenges of establishing a new congregation. The objective is to identify signs of genuine calling, godly character, spiritual resilience, and visionary servant leadership.

SAMPLE LETTER TO ASSESSORS

Below is a sample letter directed to each assessor, clarifying the importance of their role in this evaluation process and providing an overview of the assessment guide.

Sample Letter to Assessors

Dear [Assessor's Name],

Thank you for agreeing to participate in the assessment process for [Candidate's Name], who has expressed a desire to serve as a church planter. Your involvement in this vital work is critical, as it reflects the discernment of Christ's Body in identifying and supporting those called to labor in church planting ministry.

This assessment guide will lead you through a structured evaluation rooted in biblical values, ensuring our approach remains faithful to God's standards rather than the world's metrics. Your insights as a [lay leader, experienced pastor, former church planter, etc.] will help us form a comprehensive understanding of the candidate's readiness and resilience for this demanding call.

We have provided materials for your review and reflection, including a preparatory assessment package to be completed by the candidate. As you read through these documents, please note observations that resonate with the seven key assessment areas in Appendix 6 of our assessment guide. Following your review, we will gather as a team for prayerful discussion and discernment before conducting a final interview with [Candidate's Name].

Your participation, experience, and wisdom in this assessment process are invaluable, and we are grateful for your time and insights. May our efforts honor God and serve the candidate, [Candidate's Name], in ways that bring clarity and encouragement for future ministry.

In Christ,

[Your Name]

CONDUCTING THE ASSESSMENT WITH PREPARATORY ASSESSMENT MATERIALS

To aid in a thorough and prayerful assessment, we have designed a combination of preparatory materials to be completed by both the church planting candidate and selected references. These materials will guide the assessment team's discussions and provide a foundation for the final interview.

Preparatory Assessment Materials

1. Church Planting Candidate Materials:

• **Personal Testimony:** The candidate will provide a three-page testimony outlining the work of God in their life, focusing on formative experiences, spiritual milestones, and a personal sense of calling.

• **Personal Patterns and Preferences Self-Review:**

- **Written Response to the Seven Key Areas**: The candidate will answer a questionnaire related to the seven essential assessment areas as detailed in Appendix 6.
- **Life Narrative**: The candidate will outline personal patterns and life experiences in the following categories, with each response limited to three pages:
  - **Top Three Areas of Strength**: Highlight specific areas of success or accomplishment in childhood, adolescence, young adulthood, and beyond. No achievement is too small to include.
  - **Top Three Areas of Struggle**: Describe areas of past challenge, noting any lessons learned or areas where personal growth has occurred.
  - **Post-Conversion Focus Areas** (if applicable): Identify any new areas of growth, focus, or strength that emerged following conversion or a rededication to Christ.

2. **Reference Questionnaires:**

- **Personal References**: Two personal references (family or close friends) will provide written responses to questions aligned with the seven key assessment areas, helping to corroborate and expand upon the candidate's self-assessment.
- **Ministry Supervisors**: Two former supervisors in ministry contexts will respond to questions about the candidate's ministry performance, resilience, and adherence to the seven assessment areas. To maintain privacy, reference responses can be collected through a confidential online survey platform.

Each assessment team member will review all preparatory materials before convening for a private and confidential discussion meeting. This meeting will include a time of prayer and discussion, after which the team will conduct a personal interview with the candidate, focusing on questions that delve further into the seven assessment areas.

ASSESSMENT RESULTS AND RECOMMENDATIONS

The outcome of the assessment process will result in one of the following recommendations:

1 Counsel for Further Reflection: Areas needing additional reflection or growth will be noted, and specific guidance or resources may be recommended.

2 Affirmation with Suggestions: The team may affirm the candidate's preparedness in the seven key areas but suggest further reflection, prayer, or experience in one or more areas to enhance readiness.

3 Clear Affirmation ("Go" with No Further Comments): If all assessment areas are satisfied, the team will endorse the candidate's readiness for church planting ministry.

In all assessments, the team's purpose is to *uphold God's standards as revealed through Scripture and the leading of the Holy Spirit, enabling a meaningful, biblically grounded process for discerning the candidate's call. The purpose is not to "approve" or "deny approval." Assessment is a resource ministry to the candidate and family, the supervising pastor or judicatory representative, and the sponsoring local church.*

SAMPLE LETTER TO CHURCH PLANTING CANDIDATE

Dear [Candidate's Name],

Thank you for considering the call to serve as a church planter. Entering this field of ministry requires a profound commitment to the Gospel and a strong sense of God's calling. As you seek to establish a new community of believers, this assessment process is designed to help you, along with the broader church, discern and prepare for this unique calling with clarity and confidence.

Goal of the Assessment

Our goal is to provide you with studied, prayerful counsel rooted in biblical principles and guided by insights from those who have experienced the joys and challenges of church planting. This process is not intended as a final approval or denial of your readiness for church planting ministry, which will be determined by the appropriate authorities within your denomination or church. Instead, our role is to affirm areas of strength and help identify areas where further development might benefit your future work.

The Assessment Pathway

To support this evaluation, we have organized a comprehensive assessment pathway that includes the following components:

1 Preparatory Assessment Materials: These materials will be completed online through secure platforms, allowing you to respond with openness and confidentiality.

- **Personal Testimony**: This three-page testimony should focus on God's work in your life, highlighting spiritual milestones and your sense of calling to church planting ministry.

- **Personal Patterns and Preferences Self-Review**: This part includes:

    - **Questionnaire on the Seven Key Areas**: Respond to questions based on the seven key assessment areas outlined in *Deep Roots*, Appendix 6. This questionnaire will explore your understanding and experience of these core competencies.

    - **Life Narrative**: A three-page narrative identifying:

    - **Top Three Areas of Strength**: Highlight accomplishments from different stages of life, showing God's hand in developing your gifts and strengths.

- **Top Three Areas of Struggle**: Reflect on challenges or growth areas, with any lessons learned.
- **Post-Conversion Focus Areas** (if applicable): Describe areas of new growth following your conversion or rededication to Christ.
  - **Reference Questionnaires**: Two personal references and two former ministry supervisors will complete a confidential questionnaire, providing their insights on the seven key assessment areas. This input allows a fuller picture of your readiness as seen by those who know you well.

2 Online Access: Please complete the questionnaire and submit your testimony through [confidential platform name, e.g., Typeform, MailChimp, or Zoho] at [insert link]. This platform ensures confidentiality and direct access for the assessment team.

3 Interview: After reviewing your preparatory materials, the assessment team will schedule an interview to discuss your in-depth responses. This conversation will focus on areas of strength and potential growth related to church planting ministry.

4 Response and Counsel: Following the interview, the assessment team will provide prayerful, studied counsel based on the findings of the entire process. You will receive feedback that aims to affirm your call and highlight areas where further preparation may be helpful.

Moving Forward

The assessment is structured to guide you in thoughtful preparation for ministry. It focuses on biblically grounded areas vital for sustainable and impactful service. We pray with you as you take these steps and trust that God will clearly reveal His will as you engage in this process.

Please feel free to reach out if you have questions about any part of the assessment process. Your faithful dedication is a blessing, and we look forward to supporting you on this path.

In Christ's Service,
[Your Name]
[Your Title/Position]
[Contact Information]

SUGGESTED SURVEY FORMS FOR CHURCH PLANTER ASSESSMENT

Below are suggested survey forms for use with a confidential online platform (such as Typeform or Zoho) tailored to each participant in the assessment process. Each survey includes an introduction, the Seven Key Areas for Biblical Assessment in Church Planting, and a scoring scale of 1–5, where respondents can rate each area based on specific criteria.

SURVEY FORM FOR CANDIDATE

Introduction to the Candidate Survey:

Welcome to the Church Planting Candidate Assessment Survey. This form is designed to help you reflect on your personal sense of calling, patterns in your spiritual journey, and self-assessment in crucial areas identified as essential for effective ministry. Your responses will guide the assessment team in understanding your readiness and areas for further growth as a church planter. Please answer honestly and prayerfully.

Section 1: Testimony

Please share your testimony, focusing on God's work in your life, spiritual milestones, and your sense of calling to church planting (Max 3 pages in Chicago Manual of Style with cover page and a separate references page if necessary).

Section 2: Personal Patterns and Preferences

Reflect on significant patterns in your life. Provide brief responses to each area (Max 3 pages for each section).

- **Top Three Areas of Strength**: Describe three areas in which you have consistently excelled. Share examples from childhood, adolescence, and adulthood that highlight these strengths.

- **Top Three Areas of Struggle**: Describe three areas where you have faced challenges or seen the need for growth. Share examples from different life stages.

- **Focus Areas Post-Conversion or Recommitment**: If applicable, describe specific areas of growth and focus that have emerged since your conversion or recommitment to Christ.

Section 3: Self-Scoring on the Seven Key Areas for Biblical Assessment in Church Planting

Using the 1–5 scale below, rate yourself on each key area and briefly comment on each.

Scoring Scale

1 - Needs Significant Growth
2 - Emerging Competency
3 - Competent
4 - Strong Competency
5 - Excellent/Exemplary

1 Personal Sense of Call

○ Do you feel a divine compulsion toward church planting? How have you experienced confirmation of this calling?

○ **Rating:** [1–5]

○ **Comments:**

2 Affirmation by the Body of Christ

- Have other mature Christians confirmed God's calling and gifting in your life for this work?
- **Rating:** [1–5]
- **Comments:**

3 Ability to Articulate a Call to a Specific Place

- Can you clearly express why you feel called to this specific community? Have you prepared through research or ministry efforts to serve this area?
- **Rating:** [1–5]
- **Comments:**

4 Demonstrated Resilience and Endurance

- How have you shown resilience in past ministry challenges? Are you prepared for potential isolation or adversity?
- **Rating:** [1–5]
- **Comments:**

5 A Shepherd's Heart for the Flock

- Do you demonstrate genuine love and compassion for those you serve?
- **Rating:** [1–5]
- **Comments:**

6 Faithfulness in Gospel Proclamation

- How have you consistently shared the Gospel, both in public preaching and private teaching?
- **Rating:** [1–5]
- **Comments:**

7 Visionary-Servant Leadership

- Describe how you have exercised leadership that combines vision and service, especially in ministry teams or groups.
- **Rating:** [1–5]
- **Comments:**

SURVEY FORM FOR PAST MINISTRY SUPERVISORS

Introduction for Past Ministry Supervisors:

Thank you for providing feedback on [Candidate's Name] in this Church Planting Candidate Assessment Survey. Your perspective as a former ministry supervisor offers invaluable insights into his readiness for the role of church planter. Please rate him on each key area, drawing on your experience working with him. Your responses will be confidential and used solely for assessment purposes.

Scoring Scale

1 - Needs Significant Growth
2 - Emerging Competency
3 - Competent
4 - Strong Competency
5 - Excellent/Exemplary

1 Personal Sense of Call

o How strongly did [Candidate's Name] exhibit a personal conviction for ministry and church planting?

o **Rating**: [1–5]

o **Comments**:

2 Affirmation by the Body of Christ

o Did other mature Christians confirm his calling and gifting for this role?

o **Rating**: [1–5]

o **Comments**:

3 Ability to Articulate a Call to a Specific Place

o Could he articulate a specific calling to a particular community or demographic?

o **Rating**: [1–5]

o **Comments**:

4 Demonstrated Resilience and Endurance

○ *Did you observe resilience in him when faced with ministry challenges?*

○ **Rating**: [1–5]

○ **Comments**:

5 A Shepherd's Heart for the Flock

○ *Did he demonstrate pastoral qualities, care, and compassion for the congregation?*

○ **Rating**: [1–5]

○ **Comments**:

6 Faithfulness in Gospel Proclamation

○ *How consistently did he share the Gospel with others?*

○ **Rating**: [1–5]

○ **Comments**:

7 Visionary-Servant Leadership

○ *How effectively did he exercise leadership that was both visionary and servant-hearted?*

○ **Rating**: [1–5]

○ **Comments**:

SURVEY FORM FOR PERSONAL REFERENCES (FAMILY/FRIENDS)

Introduction for Personal References:

Thank you for participating in the Church Planting Candidate Assessment Survey. Your responses will provide valuable insights into [Candidate's Name] as he considers his calling to church planting ministry. Please rate each key area below based on your knowledge and relationship with him. Your feedback will be kept confidential and used solely for assessment purposes.

Scoring Scale

1 - Needs Significant Growth
2 - Emerging Competency
3 - Competent
4 - Strong Competency
5 - Excellent/Exemplary

1 Personal Sense of Call

- How evident is [Candidate's Name]'s sense of divine calling to church planting?
- **Rating:** [1–5]
- **Comments:**

2 Affirmation by the Body of Christ

- Does he demonstrate a calling and gifting that aligns with what others in the church recognize and support?
- **Rating:** [1–5]
- **Comments:**

3 Ability to Articulate a Call to a Specific Place

- Can he articulate a clear calling to this community and its unique needs?
- **Rating:** [1–5]
- **Comments:**

4 Demonstrated Resilience and Endurance

- Have you seen him persevere through trials or setbacks in ministry?
- **Rating:** [1–5]
- **Comments:**

5 A Shepherd's Heart for the Flock

- Does he show compassion and empathy for others in the church community?
- **Rating:** [1–5]
- **Comments:**

6 Faithfulness in Gospel Proclamation

- Is he faithful in sharing the Gospel and leading others to Christ?

- **Rating:** [1–5]
- **Comments:**

7 Visionary-Servant Leadership

- *How effectively does he lead and support ministry groups or teams?*
- **Rating:** [1–5]
- **Comments:**

SUGGESTED RESPONSE LETTERS

Below are the suggested template letters for each of the three possible assessment outcomes. Each letter is customized for the candidate and the supervising pastor or judicatory minister, with language emphasizing that the assessment is a tool for reflection and guidance, not an authoritative decision on "approval" or "denial." Each letter includes a sample paragraph template for providing specific feedback on areas needing further attention.

Letter to the Candidate: Further Reflection Needed

[Date]
[Candidate's Name]
[Candidate's Address]
[City, State, ZIP Code]
Dear [Candidate's Name],

Thank you for participating in the Deep Roots Church Planting Assessment process. We commend you for your dedication and faithfulness in exploring this calling and your willingness to undergo such careful evaluation. Our team has prayerfully reviewed the information provided through your testimony, self-review, references, and interview.

After thorough deliberation, we believe that a season of further reflection in certain areas would be beneficial as you continue to discern God's call in church planting. This is not an indication of disqualification but an invitation to deepen your understanding and preparedness. The assessment team's role is to support, reflect, and guide, not to issue approval or denial. We trust that God will provide clarity and wisdom through this process in conjunction with your local church leadership, in alignment with the model seen in Acts 13.

For example, we recommend additional focus on [specific area from the Seven Key Areas, such as "Resilience and Endurance"]. During the assessment, it became clear that while you demonstrated a heart for the ministry, further growth in this area would greatly benefit your long-term sustainability in a church-planting context. This might involve intentional experiences or mentorship focused on navigating opposition, spiritual warfare, and managing stress in challenging circumstances.

We encourage you to engage with your local church leaders, mentors, or trusted advisors for guidance in these areas. As always, we remain available to discuss these findings with you, should you desire.

May the Lord continue to guide and strengthen you in His service.

In Christ,
[Assessment Team Coordinator's Name]
Deep Roots Church Planting Assessment Team

Letter to the Supervising Pastor/Judicatory Minister: Further Reflection Needed

[Date]
[Pastor's or Minister's Name]
[Church or Ministry's Name]
[City, State, ZIP Code]

Dear [Pastor's or Minister's Name],

We are grateful for the opportunity to support [Candidate's Name] through the Deep Roots Church Planting Assessment process. Our team has prayerfully and carefully reviewed all assessment materials and conducted a thoughtful evaluation.

After thorough consideration, we believe that [Candidate's Name] would benefit from additional reflection and development in specific areas before advancing further in church planting. This assessment is not a judgment of suitability but a means of insight and counsel. As affirmed in Acts 13, we recognize that discernment ultimately rests with the local church or judicatory. Our role is to provide perspective that may assist in ongoing spiritual formation.

For example, we recommend [Candidate's Name] focus on growth in [specific area, e.g., "Ability to Articulate a Call to a Specific Place"]. The assessment indicated a strong general calling; however, further exploration of a specific community or demographic may strengthen [his/her] ability to articulate vision and mission effectively. Engaging in mentorship or guided reflection on this area may prove beneficial.

We hope this feedback will aid in ongoing discipleship and vocational discernment, and we remain available to discuss these findings with you at your convenience.

In Christ,
[Assessment Team Coordinator's Name]
Deep Roots Church Planting Assessment Team

Letter to the Candidate: Provisionally Affirmed

[Date]
[Candidate's Name]
[Candidate's Address]
[City, State, ZIP Code]
Dear [Candidate's Name],

We appreciate the privilege of partnering with you in the Deep Roots Church Planting Assessment process. Your commitment to seeking God's direction is commendable, and we are grateful for your openness throughout this evaluation.

After prayerful review, we are pleased to inform you that the assessment team provisionally affirms your calling in church planting while noting certain areas that may benefit from continued reflection and growth. This is not an official endorsement but a recommendation for you and your local leadership to consider in discernment. Our team's purpose is to offer support and guidance, trusting that your local church or judicatory will continue to shepherd you along this path, following the pattern of Acts 13.

One area we suggest you continue developing is [specific area, e.g., "Shepherd's Heart for the Flock"]. While your passion for ministry is evident, engaging in targeted experiences that allow you to nurture and disciple individuals more deeply could greatly enrich your church-planting journey. This might involve volunteering in a pastoral care role or shadowing a seasoned pastor.

Please know that we will keep you in prayer as you seek God's wisdom. We remain available to discuss any further questions.

Grace and peace,
[Assessment Team Coordinator's Name]

Deep Roots Church Planting Assessment Team

Letter to the Supervising Pastor/Judicatory Minister: Provisionally Affirmed

[Date]
[Pastor's or Minister's Name]
[Church or Ministry's Name]
[City, State, ZIP Code]
Dear [Pastor's or Minister's Name],

We are thankful to be involved in [Candidate's Name]'s church planting assessment journey through the Deep Roots Church Planting Assessment process. Your church's support of [Candidate's Name] has been evident and a vital part of this discernment.

Our team has prayerfully considered all materials submitted and concluded with a provisional affirmation. This endorsement is offered with the recognition that further growth in specific areas will strengthen [Candidate's Name]'s readiness for church planting. As in Acts 13, we believe ultimate approval rests with the local church and its discernment.

For example, we encourage further development in [specific area, e.g., "Visionary-Servant Leadership"]. This could involve mentoring or practical experiences focused on leading teams with a vision-driven servant's heart. We believe this hopeful growth will positively impact [Candidate's Name]'s future ministry.

We pray that these insights will be helpful to your ongoing oversight. We are available to discuss our findings if desired.

In Christ,
[Assessment Team Coordinator's Name]
Deep Roots Church Planting Assessment Team

Letter to the Candidate: Fully Affirmed

[Date]
[Candidate's Name]
[Candidate's Address]
[City, State, ZIP Code]
Dear [Candidate's Name],

We are grateful for your participation in the Deep Roots Church Planting Assessment process and dedication to seeking God's guidance. Our team has reviewed all submitted materials and prayerfully deliberated over your readiness for church planting.

We are pleased to inform you that we fully affirm your calling and believe you possess the foundational qualities needed for this work. We offer this affirmation as support, with the understanding that ultimate discernment belongs to your church leadership and judicatory, as reflected in Acts 13.

We commend your clear commitment to [mention any particularly strong area from the Seven Key Areas, such as "Demonstrated Resilience and Endurance"], which was evident throughout the assessment process. This quality and others will serve as a strong foundation as you step forward in faith.

We continue to pray for you and encourage you to keep close to the Lord as you advance in this important calling.

Yours in Christ,
[Assessment Team Coordinator's Name]
Deep Roots Church Planting Assessment Team

Letter to the Supervising Pastor/Judicatory Minister: Fully Affirmed

[Date]

[Pastor's or Minister's Name]

[Church or Ministry's Name]

[City, State, ZIP Code]

Dear [Pastor's or Minister's Name],

Thank you for entrusting us with the privilege of assessing [Candidate's Name] in the Deep Roots Church Planting Assessment process. Our team has carefully and prayerfully evaluated all assessment components and completed a thoughtful review.

We are pleased to report that we fully affirm [Candidate's Name] for church planting ministry. This affirmation recognizes his preparedness and evident commitment to the Gospel ministry. We believe [Candidate's Name] possesses the essential qualities outlined in the Seven Key Areas of Assessment, which we hope will serve as a foundation for fruitful ministry.

We particularly commend [Candidate's Name]'s strength in [mention the specific area, e.g., "A Shepherd's Heart for the Flock"], as evidenced through references and the interview process. We believe this will significantly benefit the future congregation.

We look forward to seeing God's work in [Candidate's Name]'s life and ministry and remain available for further discussion if desired.

Grace and peace,

[Assessment Team Coordinator's Name]

Deep Roots Church Planting Assessment Team

ACKNOWLEDGMENTS

No one does ministry alone. First and foremost, ministry requires the Holy Spirit, going before, guarding behind, and dwelling within. Thank You, Lord Jesus Christ, for Your constant presence, love, and forgiveness. Thank You for choosing a sinner saved by grace to bear the news of Your Gospel to the ends of the earth. I am a poor and unprofitable servant, both honored and humbled to be a little soldier in the happy service of a kind King.

My deep gratitude extends to Mrs. Christine Hartung, my former executive assistant. In one week, Christine often juggled a hundred responsibilities with grace! She managed counseling appointments, guided pastors in meetings, connected me with students, coordinated schedules, arranged travel, reviewed multiple projects, created church bulletins, and handled accounting functions—all at once! Mae and I and Faith for Living, Inc. are deeply blessed by her remarkable gifts. She is like Mark to St. Paul: "(s)he is useful to me in the ministry" (2 Timothy 4:11). Although retired from our ministry, Christine, I thank you with joy for your kind and generous support.

I am forever grateful to my son, John Michael Ellis Milton, who was primarily raised on the church planting field. As we labored to gather congregations, John became my indispensable aid, standing at the door with me each Sunday to greet the many people who passed by with a handshake and a thank you. Mostly, you helped me write and try to live out this book with your presence, support, laughter, encouragement, and, well, just by being the person God made you to be. Son, I am so proud of you.

I also offer a special note of thanks for the faithful prayers of my friend and board member, the Rev. Dr. George Grant. George has demonstrated a ministry of prayer for me and many others. Who can say what dangers were avoided, what ambushes averted, and what temptations were lifted because of such prayer? Thank you, Dr. Grant.

I must also thank my home church pastor, Rev. Robert Baxter, who has consistently modeled faithfulness in both vocation and life. His guidance has been God's chief light of wisdom for my ministry. Thank you, Pastor Bob, and thank you, Marylu.

I am ever grateful to the late Dr. D. James Kennedy, who became a mentor to me during my time as his intern. From the moment he presented the Gospel according to the Scriptures and the Holy Spirit opened my eyes to grace through faith (Ephesians 2:8-9) to my days at Knox Seminary and Coral Ridge Presbyterian Church, I was privileged to observe a life consecrated to Christ. Though he is in heaven now, his teachings remain in my heart. Thank You, Lord, and thank you, Dr. Kennedy.

Finally, I thank Mrs. Mae Milton, an extraordinary wife, mother, and faithful pastor's daughter who became a gracious pastor's wife. Mae has traveled with me through three church plants, a senior pastorate in a historic church, as a seminary leader's wife, and in ministry as an Army Chaplain's spouse. She has served alongside me in ministry, from teaching children in Chennai and visiting the sick in Chattanooga to evangelizing in Kansas City and serving in Wales. Words cannot begin to capture how much she means to me; I simply could not conduct ministry without her. Thank you, my beloved Mae. We have been richly blessed in the sacred bonds of marriage. Her presence remains the joy of my life.

———

ABOUT THE AUTHOR

Dr. Michael A. Milton (PhD, University of Wales) is a Presbyterian minister (PCA), theologian, educator, and author dedicated to equipping the next generation of Christian leaders. As a church planter, he founded three churches across Kansas, Georgia, and North Carolina, along with a Christian school in Overland Park, Kansas. He served as Senior Pastor of First Presbyterian Church, Chattanooga, TN. He formerly held the roles of Chancellor/CEO, President of Reformed Theological Seminary (RTS), and Provost of Erskine Theological Seminary. Currently, Dr. Milton is the Distinguished Professor of Missions and Evangelism at Erskine Theological Seminary and is a doctoral advisor for the Union School of Theology (UK) and the Free University of Amsterdam.

With over three decades of experience in ministry and academia, Dr. Milton brings a depth of wisdom shaped by his theological training, military service as a U.S. Army Chaplain (Colonel), and extensive pastoral and educational roles. A recipient of North Carolina's highest public service award, the Order of the Longleaf Pine, he holds a Master of Public Administration from the University of North Carolina at Chapel Hill. Dr. Milton has authored numerous works on theology, leadership, and Christian living, consistently emphasizing a pastoral approach to intellectual and spiritual engagement. A board-certified pastoral counselor, he encourages students to think critically, reflect theologically, and serve faithfully in their vocations through his teaching and writing.

Dr. Milton and his wife, Mae, live in the Blue Ridge Mountains of western North Carolina.

For more on Dr. Michael A. Milton:
- **Substack**: DrMilton.live/home
- **Website**: michaelmilton.org
- **CV, Social Media, and More**: linktr.ee/mmilton

BY THE AUTHOR

For scholarly articles, see Michael A. Milton at Google Scholar.
For magazine articles, see Michael A. Milton at Muckrack.

―――

"THE D. JAMES KENNEDY INSTITUTE OF REFORMED LEADERSHIP ESSAYS" SERIES

Milton, Michael A. *The Triumph of Mystery: Theology and Science at the Intersection of Humility and Wonder.* "The D. James Kennedy Institute of Reformed Leadership Essays #1." Charlotte, NC: Bethesda Publishing Group, 2023.

―――. *Liberty & Classism: Understanding the Political Philosophy of Leftist Elites.* "The D. James Kennedy Institute of Reformed Leadership Essays #2." Charlotte, NC: Bethesda Publishing Group, 2023.

―――. *A Theology of Learning.* "The D. James Kennedy Institute of Reformed Leadership Essays #3." Charlotte, NC: Bethesda Publishing Group, 2024.

"THEOLOGICAL HIGHER EDUCATION" SERIES

Milton, Michael A. *A Seminary Professor's Plea for Christian Scholarship.* "Theological Higher Education #1." Charlotte, NC: Bethesda Publishing Group, 2023.

―――. *The Disciple as Seminarian.* "Theological Higher Education #2." Charlotte, NC: Bethesda Publishing Group, 2024.

―――. *The Cape of Good Hope: The Chaplain as Missionary to the Secular Age.* Charlotte, NC: Bethesda Publishing Group, 2024.

"THE CHAPLAIN MINISTRY" SERIES

Milton, Michael A. *Involved with Mankind: A Theology of Chaplain Ministry.* "The Chaplain Ministry #1." Charlotte, NC: Bethesda Publishing Group, 2023.

―――. *The Pastoral Decision-Making Model.* "The Chaplain Ministry #2." Charlotte, NC: Bethesda Publishing Group, 2023.

―――. *Renewing Your Commitment to Christ's Call.* "The Chaplain Ministry #3." Charlotte, NC: Bethesda Publishing Group, 2023.

———. *Suffering for Christ: Wounds of War.* "The Chaplain Ministry #4." Charlotte, NC: Bethesda Publishing Group, 2023.

———. *Walking the Tightrope.* "The Chaplain Ministry #5." Charlotte, NC: Bethesda Publishing Group, 2023.

———. *The Cape of Good Hope: The Chaplain as Missionary to the Secular Age.* "The Chaplain Ministry #6." Charlotte, NC: Bethesda Publishing Group, 2023.

BOOKS BY MICHAEL A. MILTON

———. *Authentic Christianity and the Life of Freedom: Expository Messages from Galatians.* Eugene, OR: Wipf & Stock Publishers, 2005.

———. *Called?: Pastoral Guidance for the Divine Call to Gospel Ministry.* UK: Christian Focus Publications, 2018.

———. *Cooperation Without Compromise: Faithful Gospel Witness in a Pluralistic Setting.* Eugene, OR: Wipf & Stock Publishers, 2007.

———. *Finding a Vision for Your Church: Assembly Required.* Phillipsburg, NJ: P&R Publishing, 2012; 2nd ed., Eugene, OR: Wipf & Stock Publishers, 2024.

———. *Following Ben: Expository Preaching as the Power for Frail Followers of Pulpit Giants.* 1st ed. Eugene, OR: Wipf & Stock, 2006.

———. *Giving as an Act of Worship.* Eugene, OR: Wipf & Stock, 2006.

———. *Hit by Friendly Fire: What to Do When Fellow Believers Hurt You.* Darlington, England; Carlisle, PA: Evangelical Press, 2012; 2nd ed., Eugene, OR: Wipf & Stock Publishers, 2024.

———. *How Lovely is Your Dwelling Place: Why I Love the Church.* Charlotte, NC: Bethesda Publishing Group, 2024.

———. *Journey of a Lifetime: A Basic Guide to Discipleship for the New Believer in Jesus Christ Our Lord.* Charlotte, NC: Bethesda Publishing Group, 2023.

———. *Leaving a Career to Follow a Call: A Vocational Guide to the Ordained Ministry.* Eugene, OR: Wipf & Stock Pub, 2000.

———. *Lord, I Want to Follow Your Call: A Pastoral Guide to the Ordained Ministry.* 1st ed. Charlotte, NC: Bethesda Publishing Group, 2017.

———. *Oh, the Deep, Deep Love of Jesus: Expository Messages from John 17.* Eugene, OR: Wipf & Stock Pub, 2007.

———. *Silent No More: A Biblical Call for the Church to Speak to State and Culture.* Fort Worth, TX: Fortress Book Service, 2012.

———. *Small Things, Big Things.* Phillipsburg, NJ: P&R Publishing, 2011; 2nd ed., Eugene, OR: Wipf & Stock Publishers, 2024.

———. *Songs in the Night: How God Transforms Our Pain to Praise.* Phillipsburg, NJ: P&R Publishing, 2011; 2nd ed., Eugene, OR: Wipf & Stock Publishers, 2024.

———. *Sounding the Depths: When Jesus Prays for His People.* Evangelical Press, 2016.

———. *The Cape of Good Hope: The Chaplain as Missionary to the Secular Age.* Charlotte, NC: Bethesda Publishing Group, 2024.

———. *The Demands of Discipleship: Expository Messages from Daniel.* Eugene, OR: Wipf & Stock Pub, 2005.

———. *The Secret Life of the Pastor: And Other Intimate Letters on Ministry.* UK: Christian Focus Publications, 2015.

———. *The Triumph of Mystery: Theology and Science at the Intersection of Humility and Wonder.* "The D. James Kennedy Institute of Reformed Leadership Essays #1." Charlotte, NC: Bethesda Publishing Group, 2023.

———. *Vocation and Reform.* 1st ed. Charlotte, NC: Civitas division of Faith for Living, Inc., 2016.

———. *Vocation and Reform in Public Administration.* Germany: Grin Verlag, 2018.

———. *What God Starts, God Completes.* Updated ed. UK: Christian Focus, 2012.

———. *What Is Perseverance of the Saints?* Phillipsburg, NJ: P&R Publishing, 2009; 2nd ed., Eugene, OR: Wipf & Stock Publishers, 2024.

———. *What Is the Doctrine of Adoption?* Phillipsburg, NJ: P&R Publishing, 2009; 2nd ed., Eugene, OR: Wipf & Stock Publishers, 2024.

AS A CONTRIBUTOR:

Penny, Robert L., ed. *The Hope Fulfilled: Essays in Honor of O. Palmer Robertson.* Michael A. Milton, "Confession Out of Crisis: Historiography and Hope in the Westminster Assembly of Divines, 1643-52." Phillipsburg, NJ: P&R Publishing, 2008.

Rodriguez, Charlie, ed. Michael A. Milton, "Ronald Reagan and Religious Liberty." *Statism: The Shadows of Another Night.* Fort Worth, TX: Fortress Book Service, 2015.

Stout, Harry S., ed. Michael A. Milton, "Millenarianism." *The Jonathan Edwards Encyclopedia.* Grand Rapids: Eerdmans, 2017.

INDEX

Biblical Theology and Framework
    Old Testament Foundations ... 40-41
    Gospel Mandate ... 16, 40
    Great Commission ... 122
    Covenant Theology ... 40-41

Church Planting
    Definition and Purpose ... 15-17, 122
    Preparing for Church Planting ... 150-152
    Strategies and Methods ... 122-123
    Role of the Church Planter ... 5, 15-16, 72, 122

Church Planter Characteristics
    Visionary-Servant Leadership ... 227, 239
    Personal Holiness ... 72, 84-85
    Spiritual Gifts and Discernment ... 5, 16
    Public Proclamation ... 138

Community and Context
    Community Assessment ... 138-140
    Cultural Sensitivity ... 6, 17
    Demographic Overview ... 210-211

Spiritual Needs and Context ... 16-17, 138

Historical and Theological Influences

Apostle Paul ... 5, 122

John Stott's Preacher's Portrait ... 84-85

George Eldon Ladd's "Already and Not Yet" ... 17-18

Early Church Evangelism ... 123, 185

Pastoral Ministry

Vision and Mission Planning ... 152, 207-211

Counseling and Private Teaching ... 138, 239

Role of Elders and Deacons ... 150

Practical Aspects of Ministry

Church Naming ... 151

Strategic Planning ... 151-152

Team Development ... 227, 239

Scripture References and Reflections

Isaiah 49:6 ... 40, 41

Matthew 28:19-20 ... 40, 122

Psalm 67 ... 41

Acts 1:8, 8:8, 13:1-3 ... 17-18, 123

Spiritual Formation and Discipleship

Personal Discipleship ... 15-17

Building Faith Communities ... 5-6, 41

Gospel Conversations ... 138

Vision and Mission

Creating Vision Statements ... 151-152, 207

The "Already and Not Yet" Principle ... 17-18

Golden Lampstand Metaphor ... 17

SCRIPTURE INDEX

Genesis
1:1 - 102
2:7 - 103
12:1-3 - 50, 120
Exodus
3:14 - 45
Deuteronomy
6:4-5 - 24
Psalm
1:1 - 88
23:1 - 43, 99
46:10 - 67, 115
Proverbs
3:5-6 - 30, 119
Isaiah
6:8 - 39, 112
9:6 - 65
Jeremiah
29:11 - 91

Ezekiel
36:26 - 34
Matthew
5:14-16 - 29, 81
6:33 - 17, 101
9:37-38 - 53, 104
16:18 - 41, 78
28:19-20 - 13, 84
Mark
1:15 - 97
16:15 - 76
Luke
2:10-11 - 44
19:10 - 33, 98
John
1:1 - 59
3:16 - 49, 110
10:10 - 63, 109
14:6 - 35, 107
Acts
1:8 - 55, 92
2:42 - 61, 111
4:12 - 74, 117
Romans
1:16 - 46, 95
8:28 - 22, 66
1 Corinthians
9:16 - 57, 82
2 Corinthians
5:17 - 69, 113
Galatians
2:20 - 72
Ephesians

2:8-9 - 21, 105

Philippians

4:13 - 26, 89

Colossians

1:28 - 36, 86

1 Timothy

4:14 - 48

2 Timothy

4:2 - 77, 118

Titus

1:5 - 42, 100

2:11-14 - 31, 106

Hebrews

4:12 - 14, 80

James

1:5 - 18, 93

1 Peter

2:9 - 54, 116

Revelation

7:9 - 62, 108

www.ingramcontent.com/pod-product-compliance
Lightning Source LLC
Chambersburg PA
CBHW071242230426
43668CB00011B/1546